Richer and Poorer

The Structure of Inequality in Canada

Anton L. Allahar
and
James E. Côté

James Lorimer & Company Ltd.
Toronto, 1998

James Lorimer & Company acknowledges the support of the Department of Canadian Heritage and the Ontario Arts Council in the development of writing and publishing in Canada. We acknowledge the support of the Canada Council for the Arts for our publishing program.

Cover design: Kevin O'Reilly

Canadian Cataloguing in Publication Data

Allahar, Anton L., 1949–
    Richer and poorer: the structure of inequality in Canada

Includes bibliographical references.
ISBN 1-55028-611-0 (bound) ISBN 1-55028-610-2 (pbk.)

1. Equality — Canada. 2. Canada — Social conditions. 3. Canada —
    Social policy.

I. Cote, James E., 1953– . II. Title.

HN110.Z9S6 1998a   305'.0971   C98-930386-1

James Lorimer & Company Ltd., Publishers
35 Britain Street
Toronto, Ontario
M5A 1R7

Printed and bound in Canada

1

Canada's Dominant Ideology

Social reality is never objectively accessible to the observer. It is always viewed through a set of screens or filters. Those screens or filters are called ideologies and represent the subjectively accumulated "baggage" of knowledge and experience everyone brings to a social encounter. Ideologies mediate between the observer and the thing being observed. Nobody is free of or above ideology because, as subjective beings directly involved in making sense of our worlds, all human beings produce, and live in, a world of subjective meaning, a meaning that makes sense to them, even if to no one else.

Given this, it is clear that not all people will have the same understanding of the same event. At a football game, for example, two spectators who cheer for opposing sides will not have the same reaction to a referee's decision about a foul. A foul the referee misses is unlikely to be interpreted as a foul by the supporter of the team that commits it, but to the other team's supporter, it will be glaring. This is what team loyalty is about, and it is a reasonable way to approach the question of ideology.

As systems of beliefs and ideas that mediate contact with social reality, whether at the global or local level, ideologies are of many types and contain both psychological and sociological elements. Thus, in the football example given above, loyalty relates to the psychological "need for belonging" that all humans feel as well as to the social demands and constraints of group membership and identification. There are religious ideologies such as Christianity, political ideologies such as democracy, and economic ideologies such as free trade. White supremacy is a racial ideology, just as patriarchy is a sexual ideology.

What Are Ideologies?

Every ideology has several dimensions. Although they overlap and are mutually reinforcing, these dimensions can be analyzed separately. The first of these is the *cognitive* dimension, which is the most important to an understanding of what ideologies are and how they function. This dimension refers to the complex mix of knowledge and belief in all ideologies. It is complex because while knowledge is verifiable using logic and the scientific method, beliefs are not. Beliefs are often based on myths that in no way correspond to reality, and are accepted simply because the believer *wants* to believe them; no proof is needed. This can be seen in the religious ideology of Christianity, where the believer accepts Christ, along with such stories as the Virgin Birth, the Crucifixion and Ascension into Heaven, the Garden of Eden, and Noah's Ark.

Similarly, to understand the separation of knowledge and belief, we can look at the political ideology of patriotism during war. Consider the 1991 Gulf War between Iraq and the American-led allied forces. It is true that Iraq had invaded Kuwait; it is true that Saddam Hussein is a dictator and that Iraq is not a democratic country; and it is true that Iraq has used poison gas on its Kurdish citizens. But the Gulf War also highlights many myths about the United States: the myth that all citizens of the United States are created equal and enjoy equal freedoms; the myth that the United States is the world's leading defender of democracy; the myth that its involvement in the war was not motivated by economic and political self-interest. Further, what the myths do not say is that, before it invaded Kuwait, the United States had trained, armed and supported Iraq in its war against Iran for eight years; that Iraq's oil is vital to American prosperity and industry; that Kuwait was not, and has never been, a democratic state; and that the United States has a history of installing and supporting dictators around the world. But the average American citizen does not see these facts as relevant; nor are they ever talked about in the media, which encourage citizens to believe the myths of their country.

For a Canadian example of this separation between knowledge and belief or myth, we can look at the conquest of the Native peoples. It is true that the Natives were different from the settlers (or pioneers) and that they were perhaps hostile at times to those who invaded their lands, abused Native women, and stole their property. It is also true that the Natives did not have the same religious belief systems as the settlers. But that the "red men" were godless, that they were sly, uncultured savages, and that they attacked and scalped innocent settlers without reason, is the stuff of myth and legend. These are politically manufactured images that serve the purposes of those who benefited from the Conquest and the pillage of the Natives. Many of these images remain with us today. That is why, in any armed conflicts between the two groups, if the settlers won a battle, the history books recorded it as a glorious victory. But when the Indians were triumphant, it was deemed a bloody massacre. This is not to say that the existence of such myths is either bad or good: it is merely to acknowledge that every society is founded upon, and is saturated with, myth.

The second characteristic of ideology is its appeal to emotion and sentiment. Those who adhere to ideologies are often blindly passionate and emotional about their beliefs, and their actions can appear irrational and capricious to non-adherents. This can be seen when passions of national identity are stirred over war, where intense feelings of attachment can lead to wholesale slaughter of other human beings simply because a call to arms was issued in the name of the nation. At a somewhat less violent level, these emotions can also be seen at such events as the Olympic Games and other international sporting competitions where national flags, anthems, national colours, and various other symbols of patriotic identification and commitment are fiercely displayed and defended.

A third characteristic of ideologies is the fact that they embody value judgments. They seek either to endorse or to challenge an existing system of social relationships and institutions. When we refer to Canada's economic system as one of "free enterprise," we emphasize the great value we place on all aspects of freedom. By contrast, and sticking with the value we place on freedom in the West, American President Ronald Reagan described the former Soviet Union as an "evil empire" bent on the destruction of the "free world." The concern with "freedom" thus expressed is meant as a critique of those other social systems that are purportedly unfree and whose citizens are less fortunate than those who live in the West.

Ideologies also usually imply a call to action. If we take the ideology of feminism, for instance, it is not sufficient for an adherent to be a feminist in name only. Being a feminist means practicing gender equality and promoting it wherever possible, while combating sexism. It is rare to encounter an ideology that doesn't prescribe a course of action aimed at correcting wrongs or deficiencies in a given social system. Even the philosophy of a group that calls itself REAL Women, which is opposed to feminism and in favour of the traditional gendered division of labour, can be seen as a call to action — in this case, conservative action.

By extension, then, one can speak of conservative ideologies, which seek to maintain the status quo, radical ideologies, which attempt to overturn the status quo, and reformist ideologies, which tinker with or propose small-scale changes within the existing system. Thus, as we have said, the ideology promoted by REAL Women is conservative, while Marxist feminism is an example of a radical ideology, and liberal feminism is reformist because, instead of developing a fundamental critique of capitalism, liberal feminism in Canada merely seeks changes to help women do better within the existing set of social arrangements.

Finally, all ideologies have what is called a societal base. They are rooted in social groups and serve their interests. Individuals might hold certain ideologies, but they do not develop them; not even Marx could be said to have developed "Marxism," nor Christ Christianity. In this fashion it is possible to specify various groups in society — women, blacks, industrialists, labour unions, and so on — identify what their principal interests are and discover the ideologies associated with them. For it is in the ideology of the group that one will find its philosophy or statement of purpose, its values, and its directing motives.

In sum, therefore, we might say that ideologies are systems of emotionally charged beliefs and ideas that mediate between individuals and groups, on the one hand, and "social reality," on the other. In the process they magnify certain aspects of that reality and stress to the observer those things that reaffirm the observer's beliefs and ideas. Thus, the liberal–democrat holds the regular election of political leaders, the freedoms of speech, movement, association and so on, to be defining features of his or her society. But ideologies also mask or minimize those negative aspects of social reality that the observer is reluctant to acknowledge. So, to turn to the above example again, those aspects of liberal democracy that underline its compatibility with social inequality (e.g., ghettos, racism, sexism, youth exploitation, support for non-democratic governments and unjust wars) never figure in the liberal–democrat's description of his or her society. And, as we shall see, to the extent that they are even acknowledged at all, they are cast as non-systemic, as aberrations, or as the failures of individuals. Such aspects of liberal democracy are masked because they do not accord with the image of society that the holder of the ideology wishes to entertain or project.

Ideology, Inequality, and Order

Because inequalities in any social system have the potential of producing conflict and disrupting public order, they need to be politically managed. So, we will examine the ways in which their objective existence is dealt with ideologically in a liberal democratic country such as Canada. We will also speak to questions of power and legitimacy, as well as to the fact that, depending on the political circumstances surrounding any debate over inequality, the individual and social-structural explanations will vary. Canada is a country where white, male, Anglo-Saxon, Protestant, wealthy, middle-aged, and older heterosexuals hold power in the leading institutions (and are generally seen to do so legitimately for historical reasons). Therefore, it is these individuals and the class(es) they represent who often define the "true" nature of social inequality. These people draft the laws on behalf of the wider society, and, as a consequence, they are most responsible for shaping the ways the average citizen perceives her or his society. It therefore stands to reason that such laws, the policies they uphold, and the images they project, will be conservative.

A key strategy employed to defuse potential conflict is the attempt to explain away social inequality as a naturally occurring phenomenon. This is important to emphasize, because although we speak of *social* inequality, there are those who assume that some forms of it are *natural*. Such people tend to think and speak of the natural superiority of one race or sex over another. We know, however, that while nature might make people short and tall, black and white, male and female, and so on, the natural differences between them are simply that — natural differences. There is no such thing as "natural inequality" — it is an oxymoron! Only in *society* are evaluations made that hold that it is better to be white than black, better to be male than female, and so on.

These social evaluations are at the base of all social inequalities. To take a social contrivance — for example, the poor performance of blacks on a white-biased IQ test — and make it out to be part of the natural order of things is ideological. It masks the fact that certain privileges accrue to those with power, who are able to deflect public attention from themselves by promoting the erroneous idea that social inequalities are naturally conditioned. Since *nature* has no consciousness, motives, or intentions, the disadvantaged really have no one to blame for their predicament. Thus, in the above example of the IQ test, the wider racism of the society — which consigns more blacks than whites to inferior education, to lower paying jobs, to crime-ridden neighbourhoods and to frequent confrontations with the police — is easily cast as a racial problem and not one of class because racial problems are so much more visible than the effects of class. Blacks may be seen to be disproportionately involved in crime, but the class explanation might well be far more compelling.

The variables of gender and age could easily be substituted for race here. Race and gender have recently been high on the political agenda (though age has not) and they have tended to overshadow class. Our argument, though, is that (a) class inequality is fundamental, and (b) most other forms of inequality are best understood as deriving from class. But this does not mean that race, gender, and age are less real or less important than class. It is essential to understand both how present patterns of social inequality came about (the historical context) and the justifications (ideologies) that have been invoked by the privileged as a means of discounting them. This is the intellectual challenge to be met, and it must precede any attempt to remedy the ills of social inequality.

The people in authority have a political stake in promoting the view that inequalities in society are natural. If this is not done, if inequality is understood to be imposed by the powerful and privileged, the underprivileged could be incited to revolt. The disenfranchised are more likely to accept that theirs is a deeply divided society, while the privileged will want to nurture beliefs and ideas that seek to portray a more egalitarian view of the society. The rulers or oppressors, who have a vested interest in maintaining the status quo, dismiss the claims of the ruled or oppressed as unrealistic, "utopian," while the latter attack the authorities' views in defence of the order of things as "ideological."

The Functionalist Argument for Inequality

Another political strategy for dealing with the potentially disruptive consequences of inequality is to claim that inequality is positive and desirable. In sociology this is best represented by the functionalist school of thought, which dominated sociological thinking in the 1940s, 1950s, and part of the 1960s. According to functionalism, social inequality is a fact of life. It has existed in all known human societies and is therefore thought to be inevitable. In any society, functionalists contend, there is a wide variety of jobs that need to be performed, and some of these are understandably more important or crucial for the survival of the society in question. Further, human beings have different natural talents and abilities and, if the most talented and able are to be recruited to the most important positions, a system of unequal rewards is necessary to motivate them to pursue the types of education and training necessary for the system's survival.

In this view, unequal rewards include such things as income, power, and prestige. Doctors, lawyers, and engineers, for example, are deemed to perform more important functions than nurses, teachers, and garbage collectors. And, functionalists also claim, apart from the fact that not everyone has what it takes to be trained as a doctor or engineer (the in-born talent and ability), those who are so blessed must undergo longer periods of training and education than is necessary for a nurse, teacher, or garbage collector. To encourage the doctor or lawyer to make the necessary sacrifices and undertake the long and costly training, society must offer handsome rewards. Thus, unequal rewards, which over time can be expected to lead to various other forms of social inequality, are seen as not only inevitable, but also as good and necessary.

Herein lies the ideological message in functionalist thinking. If its logic is accepted by the poor and disadvantaged, it becomes a political weapon in the hands of the wealthy and privileged. The latter have to feel neither guilt about their comforts nor apprehension about being assailed by the majority. They do not have to answer questions about who defines the importance of different functions, about how in-born talents are measured, about the vital importance of garbage collection and other menial jobs in any society, or about the fact that privilege breeds privilege. So the children of the wealthy, who can afford the education and training, and whose parents have the appropriate social and business contacts, will themselves come to fill the "functionally most important jobs" in the future. In the meantime they will continue to derive benefits from the poor, or the "poverty industry," which generates billions of dollars worth of jobs and salaries for doctors, lawyers, judges, police officers, prison guards, social workers, and assorted governmental bureaucrats and civil servants, not to mention the ordinary people who work as cooks, cleaners, gardeners, carpenters, plumbers, and so on, in the prisons, hospitals, half-way houses and other institutions that warehouse the poor. And, poverty also ensures that there will always be individuals eager to do the dead-end, low-paying, dirty jobs that exist in any society. This theme will be revisited when we come to deal specifically with poverty in Chapter 2.

Individualism and Liberalism

To the extent that one can identify a *dominant* ideology in Canada, we would point to a combination of individualism and liberalism. By dominant ideology we mean the conventional wisdom, the taken-for-granted aspects of daily life that most Canadians can be assumed to share. But like any ideology, the dominant ideology does not have to be "true," does not have to be spoken, does not even have to be consciously acknowledged. It simply has a mass appeal and is deeply ingrained in the value and belief systems of the population at large.

Liberalism appeals to the idea of freedom and the aspirations of the French revolutionaries of 1789. In fact, their cry for *liberté,* or freedom, from the restrictions of a crumbling feudal order embodied the very sentiments and meanings conveyed by the modern-day use of the term "liberalism." Recalling the earlier discussion of the relationship between ideology and myth, we can say that the ideology of liberalism plays upon the myth of freedom and elevates it to the status of a key or sacred tenet of any civilized society. In doing so, freedom is made virtually synonymous with two other watchwords of the French Revolution: *"fraternité"* and *"égalité."* Indeed, along with freedom, fraternity and equality can be seen to comprise the core values of liberalism. But critics point out that these core values just might be contradictory, for a free society is one in which differences, especially individual differences, are permitted to flourish. This could, and does, lead to marked social and economic inequalities. Equality, on the other hand, is a levelling philosophy; it is not tolerant of differences that could lead to inequalities. We will return to this point when we examine the way liberalism deals with the contradiction.

According to some commentators, the free or liberal society is one that permits its citizens three key freedoms: free choice, free competition, and free markets. Implicit in each of these is the notion of equality. In other words, not only are people free to choose and free to compete, but this competition is among equals who supposedly have equal access to the market and equal access to the information that will enable them to make informed choices. But, in order to complete the sketch of liberalism, there is another important ideological element that must be added: individualism.

Like liberalism, individualism was born with the demise of feudal society and the rise of industrial capitalism in the West. It refers to the social and political developments that released the individual from the constraints of community and from laws based on custom and tradition. It makes the individual master of his or her own destiny and gives each one a sense of personal responsibility for the consequences of his or her actions. Individualism also acknowledges the different "rights" that modern society grants the individual: the right to free speech; the right to free association; the right to free worship; the right to own property; the right to be free from arbitrary arrest; the right to due process before the courts of law, and so on.

The supreme expression of these *individual* rights is the liberal–democratic notion of "one person, one vote." It is an equalizing philosophy to the extent that the richest and poorest individuals in such a society are purported to have an equal say in who will govern them, and according to what rules and laws. Even though ordinary citizens know that this is not necessarily so, it is part of the myth that most individuals are prepared to entertain in a liberal–individualist society such as Canada, which is presumed to be free, and a place where people are individually free to pursue their life's goals.

When Canadians describe their political system as "democratic," they presume that it is, and always has been, both free and equal. But the freedom referred to stemmed from the dismantling of feudalism and the liberation of individuals from a paternalistic system in which custom, tradition, status, and the authoritarian allocation of work were the norm. Individuals were free to move around, to leave their communities, and to work for anyone who would offer them a job, but there was nothing equal about the system. Nor is there now. In Europe, the freeing of the individual came about 100 years before the system of one person, one vote was added to the liberal society. Even after democracy was added, it still did not mean all individual citizens were equal. Many different groups within society still did not have the right to vote: women, the unemployed, the unpropertied.

Canadian Liberalism

In Canada, liberal philosophy and ideology permeate the society's thinking. (The clearest and most thorough treatment of Canada's ideological perspectives, their sources and differences, is to be found in M. Patricia Marchak [1988].) Canada is very different from the United States where the word "liberal" has negative connotations, and is at times even synonymous with radicalism and political irresponsibility. Politically speaking, Canadians see liberals as moderates, lying somewhere between the conservative right and the social democratic left. It is clear that these terms must be defined in context, for in the same way that "liberal" has two distinct meanings in the United States and Canada, so too social democracy, which is Canada's left-wing position, will not be seen as left at all in a country such as Cuba, where left means socialist. The New Democratic Party (NDP) in Canada, both federally and provincially, is firmly committed to the maintenance of capitalism, and this disqualifies it from any claim to being socialist in the strict meaning of the word. But just as the majority of Americans have no problem referring to liberals as radicals, so too most Canadians have no difficulty seeing the NDP as socialist. To use a cliché, it is all relative.

According to the liberal perspective, society is a collection of individuals, each of whom ought to be free to pursue his or her individual goals. The most efficient way of ensuring this is the "free market" system, in which government should have only a regulatory function. Coupled with liberalism and individualism are two other related core values of the system: (1) utilitarianism, according to which the pursuit of individual self-interest will produce the greatest good for the greatest number, and (2) "materialism," the relentless and seemingly unlimited drive of individuals to acquire material possessions, which in turn are used as measures of personal achievement and social success.

As we will demonstrate in Chapter 2, liberals prefer not to speak of social classes. They generally deny the existence of class divisions in society but are prepared to acknowledge that inequalities may exist between blacks and whites, men and women, young and old, and so on. Conservatives, on the other hand, readily grant that social class divisions are real, but they see them as just and proper. Theirs is an elitist position, in which the more highly placed classes are good for society. In true paternalistic style, those classes are said to look after the interests of the "less fit" classes. For their part, socialists agree with the conservatives that classes do exist; however, they do not see this as good. Instead of justifying class inequality, they advocate its eradication.

But our main concern here is with liberalism, the most extreme form of which is known as "libertarianism." Though all the main political parties in Canada are steeped in the liberal philosophy, libertarian philosophy and ideology come closest to the politics of today's Progressive Conservative and Reform parties. As the noted

Canadian sociologist M. Patricia Marchak observes, to libertarians, "social inequality is not only inevitable because people are genetically unequal, it is also desirable because the most talented provide leadership that permits others to survive." A truly liberal government, then, will not interfere with the workings of the free market system by taxing the rich to support the poor or by developing a burdensome welfare system that acts as a disincentive for the talented to exercise their talents. Instead, in its purest form, liberalism promotes the survival of the fittest and subscribes economically to the pay-as-you-go formula. Thus, those aspects of the public economy that are government controlled will be privatized and commodified, and state subsidies will be removed from such areas as health care, education, housing, transportation, and public utilities. Even such essential institutions as psychiatric hospitals and prisons can be turned over to private interests.

This is where one can distinguish among the main political parties in Canada, or among what might accurately be termed the various branches of Canada's single political party. Although they are all committed to free enterprise capitalism and subscribe to liberal philosophy and ideology, they tend to focus on different aspects of public life. For example, the privatization and commodification of social services referred to above is closely associated with the Reform and Progressive Conservative parties' sense of liberalism, while the Liberal Party, which sees *equality* of condition as unattainable, is more likely to embrace *equal* opportunity policies and to retain subsidies for economically less well-placed groups. The New Democratic Party (NDP) is close to the Liberal Party in its espousal of liberalism, but it is far more concerned with pursuing equality of condition in the long run, and it supports equality of opportunity as an interim measure. The NDP is also not averse to having the wealthy pay more taxes than the poor. But this is all to take place within the framework of free enterprise capitalism and the preservation of private property rights. Socialism, in the strict sense of the word, is not an option, even for the NDP.

Although there is a single political party known as the Liberal Party, all of the others are deeply committed to the core values, beliefs, and practices of liberalism. These incorporate individualism and egalitarianism, the sanctity of property rights, and the legitimacy of the profit motive, as well as the right to different rewards for different levels of individual talent, ability, and private knowledge. The liberal sees education as a central mechanism for the distribution of rewards: if education is a means to mobility and if it is equally accessible to all regardless of race, gender, age, or class, then those at the bottom of the social scale have only themselves to blame for their plight. This is a wonderful device for distracting the most disadvantaged in society from the sources of their disadvantage. Once they buy into the ideas of liberalism and individualism and accept that individuals have different amounts of natural talent and ability, and once they accept the claim that the system, including the educational system, is free, fair, and open, then their lack of success is simply their own fault. Of course, those who understand the world structurally and see the social system as biased along lines of class, race, gender, age, and so on, will have to be discredited as poor losers, as lazy and shiftless, or simply as political opportunists. The task of discrediting them falls largely to key socialization agencies in the society (school, church, family, and media), which embody the ideologies of, and are controlled by, the dominant classes.

Liberalism and Free Enterprise

To describe Canada's economic system as one of "free" enterprise is to betray its liberal assumptions, including the myth that the various economic actors, from the largest transnational corporations to the smallest individual entrepreneur, share a fundamental condition of freedom and equality in the marketplace. As an economic system, capitalism is founded upon a basic inequality between those who own private or productive property, such as factories, farms, businesses, and corporations, and those who do not and so must sell their labour power to the owners of productive property in order to survive. The term "private" property must be distinguished from personal property. Private property is used to generate profits by employing wage workers or charging rent to users. Personal property, on the other hand, does not generate profits. A person's car is her or his personal property. However, if the owner charged someone to ride in it, it becomes a taxi and is regarded as private property, and the owner is required to pay taxes on the income generated.

In some circumstances, social inequalities can represent a threat to social order. So, how are social inequalities perceived by, and explained to, Canadians? If Canadian society is indeed marked by entrenched and systemic inequalities, why is the population, generally speaking, so orderly?

The answers to these questions must be sought in the overlapping dominant ideologies of free enterprise capitalism and liberal democracy in Canada. Capitalism itself implies a basic, structured inequality between owners and non-owners of productive property. It assumes the existence of at least two classes with opposing interests: one that lives off profit and exploitation, and the other that depends on wages. But this type of structured inequality is not generally offensive to the population at large, owing to the widespread ideology of equal opportunity within Canada's liberal, individualist, democratic social and political system, and owing also to the confusion this ideology produces in the mind of the average citizen. Contradictory uses and understandings of the terms "democracy" and "equality" add to the confusion.

For example, during the Cold War those who lived in the West and in the so-called free world were given to believe that their forms of social, political, and economic organization were superior, morally and otherwise, to all others, especially to the Communist regimes of China, the Soviet Union, and Eastern Europe, and also to those in the poorer countries of the Third World. Free enterprise capitalism, which, as we have said, does not claim equality among its various economic actors, nevertheless implied vaguely (and incorrectly) that anyone who was hard working and wanted to get ahead had equal access to the market. The idea of "equal access" was presented in such a way as to lead people to believe that they were equal as human beings. This was ideological and illusory. Although the political system is portrayed as a free contest among equals, each having one vote to cast, the economic system is driven by competition and inequality of access to material resources. This is the essential definition of capitalism: it is a system premised upon the fundamentally unequal ownership of property and the means of production. Without that inequality, capitalism would not exist.

We also know that the economic decisions taken by major corporations and large business interests in a capitalist society will crucially affect the lives of all citizens; and herein lies a central contradiction between the political and economic claims of the system in a country such as Canada. Liberal democracy is premised on the belief that one-person–one-vote will always produce the democratic outcome of "majority control." By extension, when the economy is governed by democratic principles and involves free actors with equal access to resources, the expected result is that of a balanced social order in which decisions are democratically made in the best interest of all. The combination of liberal democracy and free enterprise is thus promoted as ideal for any society. However, the ideology masks several facts that need to be underscored.

In spite of what we are told, we know that the Canadian constitution does not require leading economic institutions to subject themselves to popular majority control. To the extent that those economic institutions influence all aspects of the daily lives of citizens, and to the extent that governments are dependent on them for taxes and job creation, among other things, they are able to dictate terms that make them independent of government management. This being the case in liberal democratic states, governments do not actually govern at all. It is the shareholders and boards of directors of major corporations who have the main say in the economic management and direction of society. As a result, the legislation passed by government (e.g., minimum wages, acceptable pollution standards, taxation levels and exemptions, interest rates, and investment incentives) must take into account the wishes of these powerful economic actors.

There is still more to criticize in the myths of equality and majority rule contained in the ideology of liberal democracy in Canada. Government ministers and leaders of political parties are not democratically chosen, in the strictest sense of the word. The prime minister or premier of a province is put forward by the members of his or her own party, as is the slate of candidates vying for political office. After the election, it is the PM or premier who appoints the Cabinet. Unless one is a member of the elected party, then, one has no voice at the party convention that chooses the leader, who then ultimately becomes leader of the government. Members of government, therefore, are not really freely selected by and from the population at large. And the costs of running a successful campaign are well above the financial means of most Canadians. Successful politicians either have a great deal of private wealth or are able to attract handsome campaign contributions — usually from the very same corporations and businesses in whose interests they are expected to act once elected. These facts are not emphasized by those who tout the superior political morality of liberal democracy.

The contradictory claims of liberal ideology are never openly acknowledged or discussed by either the rich and powerful or the mass media that have accepted the core liberal values of the culture. The limits of individualism are never questioned, equality of opportunity is assumed to neutralize or minimize the worst consequences of inherited inequalities, freedom is presumed to be uniformly distributed, utilitarianism is felt to produce the greatest good for all, and materialism is portrayed as the natural engine that motivates human beings economically. And so the average citizen, who has been socialized by the mass media, the prevailing religious institutions, the school and university systems, and narrow political discourse, falls into line. He or she is likely to endorse the social, economic, and political structure, and to justify existing inequalities. Alternatives are defined as out of the question.

Communism and socialism are premised on contrary ideological claims. They stress the importance of economic equality and seek to level economic actors by concentrating ownership of all productive property in the hands of the state. As well, communist and socialist leaders remove the political option of voting for competing candidates or parties. Communist regimes of the past were criticized in the West as being economically equal only to the extent that the majority of citizens were reduced to a basic equality in poverty. Politically, they were said to be undemocratic and afforded their citizens no political voice, so there was no political equality.

The ideological function here was clear. As bad as life might have seemed to the average person in the "free world," their counterparts in the "unfree world" were far worse off in every respect. This fuelled a deep sense of patriotism in the countries of the West during the Cold War, which continues even today. Leaders of liberal–democratic, capitalist countries are thus able to preserve their own legitimacy by trading on the emotions and sentiments of their dominant ideologies, ensuring the allegiance even of those who suffer the greatest inequalities.

The power of liberalism and individualism is brought further into play by "blaming the victim," suggesting that present inequalities are justified because if people really wanted to work hard and improve themselves they could do so. No systemic injustice explains their inequality; instead, those who do not get ahead have failed themselves. What is more, they themselves believe this to be so. Because beliefs are central to ideologies, and because they influence people's perceptions of what is real, they play a key role in people's behaviour. Political manipulation of beliefs, therefore, cannot be ignored in any effort to account for social order and social control in any society, whether liberal–democratic or not.

Along with the strategies of invoking the "communist scare" and "blaming the victim," another ideological tactic employed to deflect potential conflict can be termed "blaming nature." This involves the use of so-called science in support of racist, sexist, and ageist doctrines. As will be seen in subsequent chapters, writers such as Herrnstein and Murray claim that blacks, for example, are not as intelligent as whites because of their genetic inheritance. Similarly, Rushton and Ankney claim that women are not as smart as men; they have smaller brains and are naturally more emotional than rational. Others claim that young people are governed by hormones and subject to periods of storm and stress that require their confinement in various social institutions and their denial of certain privileges. Ideologies that use naturalistic explanations for social inequalities serve an important political function. By invoking nature and playing down the social or class roots of inequality, the privileged are able to deny responsibility for the existence of inequality. This is politically very useful, for if inequalities are not seen as natural, but rather as imposed by the powerful, making people accept them becomes much more difficult. Perception of inequality and resentment of it could easily fuel unrest and threaten to disrupt the social order.

Liberal democracy is the political counterpart of the economic system of free enterprise capitalism in Canada. And this is where the contradiction between freedom and equality is thought to be resolved. Realizing the existence of wide inequalities in society, those responsible for deflecting disaffection and manufacturing the consent of the governed masses have abandoned the myth that "all men (and women) are created equal" or share what is called equality of condition. In its place they have instituted the ideological notion of equal opportunity, which says that, even though there are extremes of super-rich and super-poor, and even though some are naturally inferior to others, the broad commitment to equal opportunity for all guarantees that everyone has the same chance to get ahead on the level playing field called the free market. To this end there are a series of laws and policies, acts, regulations, and commissions, both governmental and private, aimed at ensuring employment equity, pay equity, gender and race equity, affirmative action, and so on.

The ideological underpinnings of social inequality cannot be ignored, for, among other things, they serve the political functions of social order and control. We are referring here to a fundamental concern that arises in all treatments of social inequality: its consequences. Do human beings acquiesce in conditions of extreme inequality? How extreme is extreme? And, is social inequality an objective fact, or a subjective perception? Clearly these are empirical questions that will require empirically situated answers. For the moment, though, some theoretical reflections are in order.

Competition and Conflict

From the foregoing it is clear that competition among various groups is part of any liberal, market society, and this is not in itself a bad thing. Competition ensures a certain degree of rational planning and leads to excellence. Just as athletes get better with good competition, so too, the various producers within a competitive economy will have to strive for excellence if they are to remain viable. In the process, they seek out better raw materials, develop better production methods, and generally offer a better product for the price, and even a better price. Given the rules of supply and demand, a system of what economists call "perfect competition" will also regulate the prices sellers can reasonably charge for their product. Competition thus leads to excellence, from which the whole society can expect to benefit.

Competition occurs virtually at every level of society and at all times. People compete for jobs, credit and other financial opportunities, housing, education, consumer markets, government grants and subsidies. There is competition for votes at election time. This is a good and healthy feature of any society, so long as the competition takes place among equals, and everyone is permitted at least a token share. But when competition is perceived to be unfair, the potential for conflict is introduced.

And so, in Canada's liberal, free enterprise system, which we have argued is neither free nor equal, the managers (government, the news and entertainment media, and religious, economic, and other leaders) must create the illusion of freedom and equality in the minds of the general public. Otherwise, they face the possibility of conflict and large-scale political mobilization against the status quo. By definition, the privileged groups in any society will have an interest in avoiding conflict that might challenge their power and affluence, while the less privileged will understandably have an interest in any conflict that might upset the balance of power and improve their own position. To preserve their social privileges the managers must get to the public's consciousness and channel it in such a way that inequality is not made to seem unfair or unjust. This is where society's managers use ideology, both to reassure themselves and to convince the public of "the justice of their injustices."

Often, as the situation in Canada shows, these strategies are successful, especially when they are combined with some measure of social and occupational mobility. If such mobility is completely blocked, as in the former apartheid system in South Africa, political instability can become widespread. As long as the black majority in South Africa accepted their imputed inferiority and did not seek equality, competition over scarce resources was non-existent. For decades South Africa had a fair measure of social stability, supported by the world's leading liberal–democratic countries, such as Canada, the United States, and Britain. But as the modern age began to catch up with South Africa's fascist regime, as the "pass laws" that restricted geographic mobility and a whole series of other measures that limited occupational mobility and entrenched white power and privilege began to crumble, the pace of overall mobility quickened, and overt conflict became widespread.

Because occupational and geographic mobility are incompatible with a system of hereditary rank, once initiated, they can lead to the rapid dissolution of conventional notions of hierarchical authority and control. While human beings are capable of accepting a certain degree of myth and self-delusion, there is a point at which the discontinuity between beliefs and realities becomes too stark, and the myth is shattered.

Wide extremes in material wealth can be ideologically justified by referring to differences in personal effort and achievement *only* if a significant number of citizens experience some connection between their efforts and the rewards they receive. As a belief system, liberalism is most vulnerable whenever disparities in wealth become too great. It is therefore important to remember that when the channels for personal advancement are open and widely used, social inequity of condition can be widely accepted.

We suggest that competition will lead to conflict in a liberal–democratic, free market system where the following related conditions obtain: (a) the resources over which competition occurs are scarce; (b) access to those resources is perceived to be unequal and unfair; (c) the idea of equality is implanted among the less equal, thus raising their hopes of improvement; (d) traditionally privileged groups resist attempts to equalize the terms of competition; (e) occupational and geographic mobility have called into question traditional explanations of inequality; and (f) the liberal promises of freedom, equality, and fairness are not matched by people's everyday experiences.

Limits of Liberalism

As we have been arguing, the practice of liberalism, whether in Canada or elsewhere, is riddled with many contradictions: freedom versus equality, individual versus society, private pursuit of profit versus public good, property rights versus human rights, and so on. In all of this, the free market, where individuals meet and compete on an equal footing, is seen as the most efficient way of ensuring individual freedom, economic and otherwise. Its supporters take a very dim view of state involvement in the management of the economy. The economic philosophy of *laissez-faire* was built on the assumption that the market could regulate itself. Adam Smith's "invisible hands" of supply and demand would guard against overproduction, overpricing, and abuse of the consumer. In the process, individuals would be free to realize their dreams, but they must also be prepared to accept individual responsibility for their actions on the market.

It did not work quite that smoothly. The obvious inequalities and unfreedoms in society led to a situation in which the rich and powerful became richer and more powerful at the expense of the poor and powerless, who, over the years have grown poorer and more powerless. As a consequence, the absolute freedom of capital to pursue profit wherever it chooses, and to exploit the labour power of whomever it chooses, regardless of socioeconomic, political, or environmental consequences, had to be tempered. There were limits to growth. Since inequality of power, wealth, and prestige came to be accepted as undeniable facts of life, the poor and underprivileged needed assistance if they were to participate in the "free" market economy, and the owners of capital needed to assist them. The levels of education, skill, and intelligence of the workforce are directly related to the type of technology it can operate, which in turn is related to the type and quality of product that can be manufactured. The Canadian economy, then, is only as strong as its workforce.

An illiterate and ignorant workforce is in nobody's interest; and to participate in today's highly competitive economic markets, with their sophisticated, computer-enhanced technologies, requires a wide variety of education, skills, and training. Even at the lower levels, these come with high price tags. Who would organize such an educational system? Who would cover the medical costs for working people and others? Who would protect the weak and infirm, and those with disabilities? Who would assure affordable housing for the poor? In short, who would be responsible for defending the most disadvantaged in the "survival of the fittest" contest that a true free enterprise, capitalist system implies? Who would pay for it? And how?

The answers lay in the creation of the welfare state and the massive public service. This was a state that had a direct economic stake in the provision of public education, public health care, the setting of a minimum wage, the regulation of profits, pollution, and environmental degradation, and the development of legislation aimed at fair employment practices and equal opportunities for all citizens. The welfare state also grew to be the major employer of labour in leading industrial societies. Governments in Canada (as elsewhere) became directly involved in banking and other financial investments, bought outright or had controlling shares in certain resource-based industries, developed numerous marketing boards and controlled Crown corporations such as the post office (federally) and Ontario Hydro and the Ontario Lottery Corporation (provincially). And it is all paid for with tax dollars.

At the dawn of the new millennium, the liberal state and society globally find themselves under serious attack, not so much from their traditional rivals on the left, as from the "new" right. By "left" we mean socialist, as opposed to social democratic, forces. Social democrats, we have already argued, simply represent a subvariety of liberals. The socialists, however, are rather silent since 1989 following the collapse of the Berlin Wall and the subsequent disintegration of the Soviet Union, not to mention the return of capitalism to Russia and its cautious welcome in China.

The new right is a powerful and fast-growing neo-conservative movement, most clearly identified in the United States with Christian fundamentalism and the so-called moral majority. It stresses corporate or collective sentiments as opposed to individualism, embraces biblical teachings and admonitions, and is highly critical of the liberal society and its value system. In Canada, it is best exemplified by the Vancouver-based Worldwide Church of God and its very influential publication, *The Plain Truth*.

The new right blames all the ills of modern society on the liberal state and its commitment to freeing the individual and granting a host of individual political rights without demanding reciprocal responsibilities. Thus, it blames liberalism and the practices of the liberal state for the following: high rates of bankruptcies and business failures, soaring unemployment and underemployment, declining belief in God, family disintegration and a lack of respect for parents and authority figures, a vanishing sense of patriotism, drug and alcohol abuse, soaring violent youth crime, exorbitant school dropout rates, epidemic levels of teenage pregnancies and routine abortions, and even poverty. Too much reckless power has been invested in the individual, and this has led to a society of chronic complainers where several generations of people on welfare confidently demand hand-outs from the state, are quick to claim their rights have been denied or violated, and are eager to sue the authorities.

To the new right, the excesses of liberalism are responsible for "political correctness," which allows fringe groups and disaffected individuals to feel politically empowered to demand redress. Along with the state, the main institutional targets of the new right are universities, the mass media, and labour unions. Universities, they feel, have grown too large and are too costly. Further, they provide a safe environment to question the sanctity of tradition and to criticize privilege. The social sciences, arts, and humanities, where little of practical value to society is learned, but where students are taught to be irresponsible, are the main offenders. The news media are seen as responsible for challenging government through investigative reports that expose corrupt politicians and religious authorities, and for calling into question the contradictions of the democratic process and undermining confidence in the system and its elected guardians. And, the entertainment media glorify violence, sex, drugs, and a way of life that goes counter to the values of community, tradition, and God. For their part, unions are blamed for pampering labour, protecting inefficiency, and ruining the competitive ethos so necessary to drive the system of free enterprise.

The new right is uncompromising in its attack on welfare sector civil servants, women and single mothers, minorities, unemployment insurance and the unemployed, minimum wage legislation, rent controls, the handicapped, and unions. It generally speaks *for* big business, but can also be seen to speak *to* the poor about their need for restraint and sacrifice, as did one British Columbia cabinet minister: "Having programs in support of single mothers causes mothers to be single and need support" (Marchak 1988:190).

Conclusion

The system of free enterprise and welfare capitalism in Canada is experiencing a deep crisis of legitimacy. It has produced and ossified certain forms of inequality that are now turning in on the system.

Internally, it faces criticisms and challenges from average citizens, from the traditional left, and from the new right. The liberal–democratic ideology made promises of freedom and equality, and the people are now asking that society deliver on those promises. But politically, economically, and even morally, the system is appearing to falter. Canadians, however, are still firmly committed to the liberal philosophy, even if its practice is not without contradictions and reversals. Its attractiveness lies in the fact that it holds out hope and acknowledges that the system is not perfect, but at the same time suggests that it is perfectible.

Thus, on the eve of the new millennium, as the country continues to wrestle with the uncertainties of global restructuring, the challenge of perfectibility is there to be taken up by all Canadians. But they must first address what we have identified as four of the most pressing forms of inequality. These relate to class, "race" (ethnicity), gender, and age (youth).

2

The Myth of the Classless Society

Canadians like to think of themselves as a "nice" people, not given to extremes. For examples of racial apartheid they like to point to South Africa, never at their own system of reserves for Natives. Poverty and hunger are to be found in India and Africa, never in the Maritimes, Northern Ontario, or even in the ghettos of our large cities. In foreign policy, the former Soviet Union, and at times even close allies such as the United States and Great Britain, are criticized as political and economic bullies, but Canadians are usually less eager to draw attention to the nefarious activities of the First Canadian Airborne Regiment in Somalia or the exploits of Canadian banks and multinational corporations in the Third World.

This is all quite understandable. People cannot be expected to portray themselves or their societies in unflattering terms. Thus, based on a 1977 survey of ethnocentric attitudes among Canadians, well over 60% of the population felt that "Canada may not be perfect, but the Canadian way has brought us about as close as human beings can get to a perfect society" (Driedger 1989:328). In other words, although most Canadians agree that ours is not yet a perfect society, we see it as *capable* of perfection, and until that time arrives, we take comfort in knowing that it is certainly better than most others; and we are correct. According to the United Nations *Human Development Report*, which ranks countries in terms of progress made towards the overall improvement of the lives of its citizens on a variety of social, economic, political, health and nutritional indices, Canada is the best country in the world in which to live. Over the past six years (1992–7) it has ranked first five times and second once (to Japan in 1993) on the "Human Development Index."

By any measure, this is an enviable record; and it is one, among many others, that gives Canadians reason to be proud. It also predisposes us to view our society in rosy terms, as being devoid of major divisions and disparities, as being generally classless. This feeds the liberal ideology that embraces the idea of equality and eschews attempts to characterize ours as a class-divided society. In this chapter (and the rest of the book generally), however, we will challenge the view that class analysis is no longer relevant to a society such as Canada's, and we attempt to bring class back into focus.

Accounting for the Myth of Classlessness

When Canadians are asked to identify their class affiliation they are likely to answer either that there are no classes in Canada, or, in order to avoid standing out from the "majority," to identify themselves as middle class. This is a curious contradiction, a seeming willingness to engage in self-delusion. Surely most Canadians are aware of the existence of great differences in income, lifestyle, and power. The key question, then, is how are those differences accounted for by the average citizen who is uncomfortable with thinking of his or her society in class terms? The answer lies in the liberal ideology, which explains social inequalities as stemming from individual effort (or lack thereof), and not from structured class relations. Self-delusion and the myth of classlessness are not difficult to understand in a consumer society where material possessions and some degree of mobility are within the reach of the average citizen. Also, the theme of individualism runs through popular stories about stout-hearted pioneers and intrepid fur traders in a rugged land, and about those of humble origins who have risen to the top by dint of hard work. It is also the stuff of history books, television movies, and common political commentary.

As a popular historian, Pierre Berton is an ideal representative of this type of myth making. Such books as *The National Dream* and *The Last Spike* have romanticized the past and fuelled a powerful blend of nationalism and individualism in the average Anglo-Canadian. They also tend to distract from class aspects of conflicts that have marked the country's history (settler versus Native, French versus English, the Métis Rebellions led by Louis Riel), in favour of cultural and ethnic explanations premised on the savagery of the Natives, the intransigence of the Métis people, and the noble efforts of settlers who tamed a wild frontier. By downplaying class, these histories and myths paint a picture of a benevolent colonial past in which "cultural differences" were amicably settled and all parties joined in common purpose to build a united Canada. To speak of class inequality in Canada and to imply that behaviour is somehow determined or structured by "invisible" class forces is held to be a denial of the basic freedoms and openness that are hallmarks of the system. This is why, in the public mind, class-based explanations of behaviour are generally resisted.

The fact is, however, that there are many class and economic inequalities in Canada, some more glaring and consequential than others. The problem for the liberal, though, is that where classes are deemed to exist they automatically imply the existence of domination, exploitation, and conflict. It is quite revealing to note what Canadians, who typically deny the existence of class, see as the recipe for advancement in life. In a 1996 study that sought to assess the requirements for "Getting ahead around the world," Carleton University political scientist Jon Pammett compared some of the leading capitalist countries (Canada, Great Britain, the United States, and West Germany). He found that "individual drive and initiative" were the most important factors identified by respondents from all countries (see Table 2.1). Specifically, Canadians ranked *ambition*, *good education*, *hard work*, and *natural ability* as the major keys to success. This fits neatly within the liberal–individualist ideology according to which individuals are largely, if not solely, responsible for their life situations, and individual characteristics are perceived as the most important determinants of any patterns of inequality that do exist.

Pammett made no attempt to tie "good education" to class background and paid no attention to those who might work hard and still not have much to show for it, and in his study the notion of "natural ability" is never examined. The enjoyment of class privilege is treated simply as a matter of luck: "Giving a boost to this personal initiative and achievement would be *the luck involved* in being born into a wealthy or well-educated family" (Pammett 1996:72; emphasis added).

Invoking the notion of "luck" here is of particular relevance to the discussion of ideology and social control. As soon as individuals begin to explain their subordinate positions in society as a function of "bad luck," or as having been dealt a rotten hand by "nature," the task of social control is virtually complete. By removing responsibility for their condition entirely from the realm of human agency, those in control, those who promote the idea that luck and fate can explain social advantage and disadvantage, escape unscathed. The ideology of classlessness persists and the status quo is left intact.

Table 2.1

Most Important Factors for Getting Ahead: Canada, Great Britain, United States, Germany 1987 and 1992

Important Factors	Canada	Great Britain		United States		West Germany	
	1992*	1987	1987	1992	1987	1992	1987
INDIVIDUAL							
Ambition	1	2	3	1	2	2	2
Natural ability	4	4	4	4	4	3	5
Hard work	3	1	1	2	1	4	4
Good education	2	32	2	3	3	1	1
CONNECTIONS							
Know right people	5	5	5	5	5	5	3
Political connections	8	11	11	7	8	8	9
Political beliefs	11	10	13	11	12	9	11
BACKGROUND							
Well-educated parents	6	6	6	6	6	6	6
Wealthy family	7	7	7	8	7	7	7
DEMOGRAPHICS							
Gender	9	9	9	9	10	11	10
Race	9	8	8	10	9	10	8
Religion	12	13	12	12	11	12	12
Region	10	12	10	12	13	13	13

* no 1987 data are available for Canada.

Source: Pammett (1996: 70).

The Political Psychology of Control

In Chapter 1 it was argued that a society characterized by extremes of wealth and poverty would likely be unstable. But in Canada, a country in which great wealth exists alongside abject poverty, instability is not much in evidence. Why is this so? The answer lies in the fact that the dominant ideology of liberalism manages to mask reality and convince citizens that they live in a middle-class society with few extremes. The dissonance produced when official ideology does not accord with perceived reality is thereby eliminated, for there is no problem if citizens are given reason to believe the claims embodied in the public ideology and if the public presentation of the "facts" accords with the internal realities of private life. The manufacture of consent by those in control of the dominant institutions must therefore aim at getting members of the society to see and interpret the evidence or facts of inequality in a manner that is not likely to be disruptive of the social order.

As we will see, this idea, or more accurately, this illusion of "mobility," is a crucial part of the engineering of control and stability in Canada. It is integral to the discussion of class and to the common confusion between class and occupation that we so often see.

Class and Occupation

For sociologists who studied the patterns of inequality in the early phases of capitalist development, the notion of class was a fairly uncomplicated one. People could be easily identified by what they did, and the economic roles of merchants, traders, factory owners, planters, slaves, factory workers, landlords, peasants, and so on were clear and largely distinct from one another. Class assumed a primary economic character that reflected the relatively simple and clear-cut divisions of labour at the time.

With the further development and sophistication of capitalism, however, the picture began to change and the political aspects of various economic undertakings became salient. Colonial law gave certain political rights to favoured classes, labour unions gained legitimacy, and governments began to play a more active role in regulating the economy. Planters became heavily indebted to merchants (who also served as sources of credit), and sold their properties to them and the merchants became merchant-planters; slaves were emancipated and converted to wage workers with very different legal rights and responsibilities; peasants became integrated into the system of market exchanges and produced both subsistence and cash crops; landlords became capitalists, and capitalists became landlords; and with the development of corporate capitalism and the rise of joint stock companies, capitalist owners, managers, and workers, all of whom could own stock in the company, started to blur the lines of class demarcation. There followed developments that saw one individual owning 10% of one company, 30% of another, and 60% of yet another. It was no longer a simple matter to identify what people did and deduce their class affiliations on that basis.

But the matter is even more complex than this. For example, it is not possible to argue that two carpenters who each make $40,000 belong to the same class simply because they both do the same type of work and make the same amount of money. If one is the owner of a small carpentry business and the other is an employee of a large carpentry firm, they may very well have the same level of income, but they will have quite different class and economic *interests*, different legal liabilities, and very importantly, different *political* orientations to capital and labour. To begin to analyze class inequality, then, we must first agree on a definition of class that (a) is applicable to the modern era of capitalism in Canada, (b) takes into account the complexity of contemporary occupational specializations, and (c) goes beyond the purely economic to embrace the political dimension of class identity and action.

Marx, Weber, and Class

Two of the most influential sociological approaches to class are those developed by Karl Marx (1818–1883) and Max Weber (1864–1920). Our definition of class will begin with Marx and then incorporate Weber's contributions, which build on Marx, and which are able to broaden Marx's treatment of the topic, given that Weber lived in a later period of capitalist development and witnessed changes Marx could not reasonably have foreseen. We are convinced that a critical integration of the class treatments of these two figures is far more advantageous than subscribing to the facile political oppositions that later commentators have constructed to divide Marxian and Weberian sociology.

This is not to say, however, that Marx and Weber were political soulmates. We do not wish to give the impression that Marxian and Weberian sociology are always and everywhere compatible, or that they even share a common political vision for society; far from it. Marx wanted capitalism to be replaced by socialism, which he felt would be more humanistic, while Weber was most pessimistic about the promise of socialism. The latter felt that as bad as capitalist bureaucracy was, socialist bureaucracy would be far more confining. Thus, while they both had serious criticisms of capitalism they did not advance the same solutions to its ills, and Weber's eschewing of radicalism is far more appealing to the liberal and in keeping with the general Canadian denial that theirs is a society of class divisions.

As a humanist, Marx was concerned with the elimination of capitalism, which he felt dehumanized workers and other subordinate groups and classes. A general improvement in the living and working conditions of the working class, the most numerous segment of the society, was Marx's goal, and so his treatment of class was bound up with his theories of revolutionary social change. In Marx's discussion of capitalism, class was understood primarily as a function of property ownership. He felt that the basic class distinctions were those between the owners (bourgeoisie) and the non-owners (proletariat) of private or productive property. It is important to point out that Marx never saw capitalism as comprising only two classes. For him the bourgeoisie and the proletariat were merely the principal or defining classes of capitalism.

Ours is a structural understanding of class, and we are primarily concerned with the ways in which classes relate to one another. By this we mean that class is a relational concept; classes only exist *in relation to* other classes. Thus, one can only speak of a ruling class to the extent that there is a ruled class over which it exercises domination. Classes, therefore, are seen as "empty places" (structures) that are only incidentally occupied by specific human beings. So we are less concerned with the actual human beings involved than we are with the structured relations among the classes.

Under capitalism, ownership of property is integral to class structure. Property rights are legal rights, enforced either by society or the state, by either custom or law. To this extent, property is an accepted social contract or agreement that sets and maintains specific relations between people. As W. Clement put it, property "is *the right [to] control the use or benefit to which ownership is put* ... [Property] is *the right to the use or benefit of things, tangible or not, enforceable by law.* This is why Marx argued that property and class relations were synonymous. If the law protects property as a set of rights as described above, it will defend one segment of society to the detriment of another. The law, therefore, which can legitimately call upon state apparatus (e.g., courts, judges, police, and prison guards) to enforce property claims, finds itself in a structural contradiction between its commitment, on the one hand, to fairly represent all classes in society, and to defend only those with claims to property on the other hand. Thus, Marx also described the state in capitalist society as a class state. Class and property are intricately intertwined, and Marx felt that the only way to abolish class and class privilege was to abolish the private ownership of property.

The fact that private property guarantees the right to control the fruits of ownership, tangible as well as intangible, has implications for the labour of non-owners of property. Thus, when the survival of the non-owners compels them to work for those who have accumulated capital and who own property, the owners are said to have a *legal right* to the labour of the non-owners. By extension, it stands to reason that those who own no private property, the workers, will have no property rights or legal claims on their employers. As was discussed in Chapter 1, private property is property used to generate income (such as lands, farms, factories, capital, and machinery), and is not to be confused with personal property such as one's car or one's house, things that are used purely for personal ends. Thus understood, "property" is particularly important in light of the legal rights it confers upon its owners.

Clearly the entire system, whose sole *raison d'être* is the pursuit of profit, will be geared legally to the exploitation and alienation of the worker. There is no such thing as "capitalism with a heart," for the capitalist who fails to compete effectively, to produce quality goods at the lowest possible cost, to corner the market and get the upper hand on competitors, will not be a capitalist very long. The idea, then, is to get as much product out of the worker for as little pay as the society and the law permit. This is the idea of exploitation, which is intimately tied to the process of alienation: workers' loss of control over (a) their own labour power, (b) the fruits of their labour, and (c) the very conditions under which they labour.

The basic division between owners and non-owners is very general and does not capture the complexities and variations in the actual amount and kind of property owned. It makes little sense to argue that a person who owns a factory, employs 150 workers, and produces a million dollars worth of commodities each year, is in the same class as one whose factory employs 15 workers and produces a mere hundred thousand dollars worth of commodities. The economic risks associated with the former enterprise are far greater, as are the amount of profits and the economic and political reach of the

Table 2.2

Basic Economic Criteria for Class Position

	Bourgeoisie	Petite bourgeoisie	Proletariat
LABOUR POWER			
Sale of	No	No	Yes
Purchase of	Yes	No	No
CONTROL OF LABOUR			
One's own	Yes	Yes	No
Others'	Yes	No	No
SOURCE OF LIVELIHOOD			
Wages	No	No	Yes
Capital	Yes	No	No

Source: Wright and Perrone (1977:34).

owner. As a defining feature of class, therefore, property ownership is a variable category which also brings with it variations in the degrees of power and control over (a) the means of production, (b) the labour process, and (c) labour itself; property grants autonomy in decision making, puts the owner in the position of exploiter instead of exploited, and enables the owner to avoid the alienation that non-owners face.

Marx was fully aware that the use of mere ownership of property as the sole criterion for class membership was insufficient. He therefore added another class to the basic bourgeois–proletarian dichotomy: the petite or petty bourgeoisie. This class's ownership of capital and productive property qualifies it as bourgeois, but its scale of operation is smaller, and its professional and managerial sectors exercise less power and control over the economy than large-scale capitalists. Nevertheless, as we will see later, the petty bourgeoisie occupies a crucial place in the Canadian class structure. This is the so-called middle class to which so many Canadians claim membership, and it is made up of small business proprietors, independent commodity producers such as farmers, artisans, and other self-employed persons, and those in the management and professional sectors.

At this point, it will be useful to introduce Weber and some of the modifications he offered to the basic Marxian schema of classes. Accepting the fundamental Marxian position that property ownership is a key feature of class identification, Weber went on to examine some of the other significant aspects of class in modern society, where the vast majority are propertyless. He focused in particular on power and the fact that there are non-economic (non-property) sources of power. For Weber power was simply the ability to issue a command and have it obeyed, even if it goes against the will of the person or persons commanded to execute it. Power, and the legitimate use of it, which he called authority, is inherent in the bureaucratic structure of modern society. Those who are wealthy and own vast amounts of property are not necessarily the only or the most powerful people.

The Prime Minister of Canada offers a good example. He is ostensibly the most powerful person in the country, yet his power does not reside in his wealth or property holdings. Rather, it comes from the bureaucratic structure of the political process, which gives political power to individuals on the basis of such things as cultural capital: their level of acquired skill, knowledge, and formal education, their peer-acknowledged accomplishments in their chosen field, their communication ability and charismatic or public appeal, and the general scarcity or availability of these qualities on the open market. That the Prime Minister is privately wealthy is incidental to the fact that he wields such great power. Less extreme examples will involve ministers and deputy ministers, university presidents, and even union leaders. Governments, universities, and unions are all bureaucratically structured organizations, and in order to move up in them, educational credentials, skill and knowledge, cultural capital, and other personal attributes are more relevant than property ownership or large bank accounts.

This is not to say, however, that property and wealth are not *necessary*; instead, it is to acknowledge that, in a critical analysis of power in the modern, bureaucratic world, they are not *sufficient*. In today's society, life generally goes on in large, formal, bureaucratically structured organizations where power is supposedly won in an open, competitive contest. We are born in hospitals, educated in schools, worship in churches, work in offices, join unions, vote for politicians, and our children play little-league sports. Each of these activities is hierarchically structured: power flows from the top down and decision making rests with managers, principals, bishops, presidents, bosses, captains, and so on. All these people supposedly derive their status and power from their knowledge and ability to help the organization reach its stated goals. They wield varying amounts of power bestowed on them by the position or office they hold in the bureaucratic structure, so they are able to command different incomes.

In such a system, a privately wealthy individual, for example, who hires an unqualified son or cousin as her accountant or business manager will not survive in the cut-throat market economy when pitted against others who hired qualified accountants or business managers on the basis of their education, skill, and knowledge. Henry Veltmeyer, a sociologist at St. Mary's University, notes that only about 25% of the corporate elite, those who really oversee and run the capitalist economy, come from the most privileged upper class. Most came from certain law firms, universities, and other institutions that serve to guarantee, in place of membership in the upper class, a commitment to its core values. While it is true that money can buy a superior education, it does not always work this way. Many who hold very powerful and prestigious positions in society come from humble or modest backgrounds. One recent study has shown that almost 35% of Canada's corporate elite come from the middle class, and over 5% from working-class backgrounds. Within the Canadian bourgeoisie, analyst Dennis Forcese shows, there is a measure of mobility; but is it as free as we are generally given to believe (Forcese 1997:55)? Or is it illusory and ideological, not what it seems?

In outlining Weber's logic we have moved our focus from Marx. The distinctions we are beginning to make have more to do with people's occupational statuses than with their class affiliations. Critics on the left view these distinctions as ideologically conservative and see those who follow Weber as resisting the controversial and highly politicized term "class" that is associated primarily with Marx. In place of "class" such Weberians prefer Weber's notion of "status" which is supposedly achieved simply by changing one's pattern of consumption and one's lifestyle. And those critics are probably correct. The challenge, however, is to combine class and occupational divisions in our discussion so that we can use the variety of occupational distinctions that characterize contemporary society not only to describe the society, but also to help explain its workings. To do so we will retain the Marxist definition of class and use Weber to distinguish occupational groupings within classes. Whereas Marx looks at class as it is linked to property and exploita-

tion, Weber observes how occupational status and prestige are distributed throughout the society, and thereby avoids having to deal
with the inherently conflictual nature of class relations. The political
implication of adopting a pure Weberian understanding is that it
tends to portray modern capitalism and its managerialist ideology in
softer terms as a type of society in which individually achieved
occupational mobility is a matter of personal effort and simple gradations in income.

The *hired* accountants or business managers of a small firm or a
multinational corporation are *employees* of capital; they are technically non-owners of property, non-capitalist in terms of their class.
But they are powerful, well-paid, and enjoy high status. So how do
we reconcile the Marxian and Weberian approaches in this analysis?
Without becoming too technical, we propose to rely on Marx's categories of bourgeoisie (the capitalist class), petty bourgeoisie (the
middle class), and proletariat (the working class), as designating the
principal *class divisions* in society, with all their economic consequences and political implications. We use Weber to talk about
occupational differentiation within the classes. Our purpose here is
not to set up a political and ideological contest between Marx and
Weber, but rather to bring class back into the analysis of social
inequality in Canada and to examine the ideological aspects of such
inequality. Thus, one of our concerns will be to see the extent to
which occupational differentiation is used by those in authority, and
accepted by the average citizen, as proof of Canada's open class
system. We will contend that, to the extent that there is mobility, it
is occupational, not class based.

The Capitalist Class or Bourgeoisie

The capitalist class, or what Marx called the bourgeoisie, can be
subdivided into several sectors depending on what one wishes to
highlight. One of the more traditional divisions contrasts the big,
resident Canadian monopoly capitalists with the far less powerful
fraction of capitalists who are junior partners of foreign (mainly
U.S.) capital. Within the Canadian capitalist class, there are industrial, financial, and commercial sectors, whose dominance is well
established in such areas as banking and insurance, transportation,
utilities and real estate, media and telecommunications, mining, im-
port, export, and retail sales. Ignoring for the moment the considerable influence of foreign capital on the economy, these are Canada's

monopoly capitalists, who, together with their executive assistants, control the lifeblood of the country.

Although it is not directly relevant to our present analysis, it is important to point out that we are not dealing here with a homogeneous capitalist class. Each of these sectors can be broken down along such lines as *extent* of economic ownership, *scope* of operations, *amount* of control of a given enterprise or area of the economy, *degree* of autonomy in decision making, management and direction of the enterprise, and so on. However, since there is a great deal of sectoral overlap in both their operations and the patterns of ownership and control, and since our main aim is simply to describe this class, we will speak of the capitalist class as a whole.

At its most extreme, the capitalist class comprises the super-rich and powerful families in Canada, what Peter C. Newman has written of in *The Canadian Establishment*. It includes such names as the Bronfmans, Thomsons, Desmarais, Westons, Irvings, Eatons, Reichmanns, and Blacks. In numerical terms, the super-rich do not exceed 2% of Canada's population and there is a core group of fewer than one thousand that owns outright 80% of all corporate stocks and bonds in the country. The extreme lifestyle of this group is never visible to ordinary Canadians: their private yachts, private clubs, private deals in private boardrooms, private jets to private destinations, and most importantly, their huge private profits, insulate them from public gaze. This is why most Canadians are able to think them away so comfortably when constructing their image of a classless society. As we will see, their "invisibility" as a class in the public mind is matched only by the "invisibility" of the super-poor.

While reliable data on the combined wealth of the Canadian capitalist class are not easily available, few will doubt the immense fortunes they command. It has been estimated that only twelve families and five conglomerates control one-third of all corporate assets in Canada, while eight corporate conglomerates control about 80% of the 300 companies listed on the Toronto Stock Exchange. It has also been estimated that, in broad class terms, the Canadian population is made up of 26.5% middle class, 63.7% working class, 8.7% lower class (including the poor and unemployed), and a mere 1.1% upper class. (Russell 1994:78)

The inordinate economic might of the capitalist class, and its ability to affect the economy as a whole, is central to any assessment of social inequality in Canada. But since economics alone does not tell the full story of control and is not the only dimension of inequality, it is equally important to stress the *political* clout of this class. Because of their family connections, huge campaign contributions, their employment of such a large part of the workforce, their ability to move huge sums of money in and out of the country and affect national interest rates, and even the overall employment levels, no government can afford to ignore the demands or wishes of this class. So it is not difficult to accept the fact that wealthy capitalists will also have direct links with political elites and decisive input into the governance of the country. For, linked in a complex pattern of social and familial relations, intercorporate ownership, and joint directorships on the boards of various corporations, these large capitalists can elevate themselves to political power and so control the state apparatus. They form an invisible government, what Marxists call "the ruling class." All of this calls into question the notions of political democracy and equality that are the cornerstones of Canada's liberal ideology and philosophy.

A perfect example of the implications of such power and control was reported by Diane Francis in *Controlling Interest: Who Owns Canada?* It relates to a former New Brunswick premier, Louis Robichaud, who recalls a conversation with a son of billionaire K.C. Irving: "My father never lost a New Brunswick election in his life," the son boasted, although everyone knows that he had never sought political office. "But for years," Francis continues, "Irving could make or break politicians" in a province where "the Irving family virtually *is* New Brunswick's private sector."

With the rise of corporate capitalism it is quite difficult, if not pointless, to try to identify the actual owners of the largest corporations, or to separate the class interests of the owners from those of their surrogates: directors, vice presidents, chief executive officers, chairpersons and managers. For in the modern corporate world it is often the case that owners are also employees of a business, and top managers own corporate stock, earn shares as part of their regular pay, and sit as directors on corporate boards. Industrialists, financiers, and managers are simply fragments of the capitalist class and can be expected to act in concert to protect and advance their common long-term interests.

Trying to trace direct ownership becomes very tangled, because a parent company is often owned by one or more finance or investment companies that are themselves owned by other finance companies. And the parent company in question can own 20, 50, or 100 other companies, each of which can own, fully or partially, another hundred or so companies, which again can own, fully or partially, other member companies, and on and on. In the age of multinational or transnational capitalism and globalization, ownership patterns have become amazingly intricate, and increasingly concentrated in fewer hands. Diagrams 2.1 and 2.2 show the widely diversified 1996 assets of the Bronfman family — a case in point.

The Bronfmans are a Canadian dynasty that in 1983 controlled some 700 companies with combined assets of over $56 billion. And while not all the country's corporate empires are family controlled, such empires are not unimportant. In 1983, for example, six families (Weston, Black, Desmarais, Irving, Thomson, and Bronfman) owned or had control of more than 1300 of Canada's largest corporations. Today, the Bronfman family is represented by two trusts: the Peter and Edward Bronfman Trusts and the Charles and Edgar Bronfman Trusts. In the late 1980s, Edper Investments, which owned or controlled 184 companies, gave the Bronfmans 41.5% in powerful Brascan, which itself had a 39.2% share of Noranda, which in turn controlled 154 companies and had a 41.1% share of MacMillan Bloedel with its 27 companies, and so on. Formerly known as the Brazilian Traction, Light and Power Company, Brascan became a true mega-corporation with an agglomeration of assets and liabilities that ranged from Rio de Janeiro's plush, five-star Hotel Intercontinental to the Toronto Blue Jays baseball club, Laura Secord, the Great Canadian Soup Company, and the Great Lakes Power Corporation. Its board members also sat on the boards of, and thus controlled, such corporate powerhouses as Norcen, Trizec, Consumer's Gas, Noranda, Hiram Walker-Gooderham and Worts, Dofasco, and Liggert and Myers, among many, many others.

All of this led analyst Diane Francis to comment that Canada's exceedingly high degree of economic concentration means that "everything from your glass of orange juice in the morning, to the clothes you put on, to the office where you work, to the department store and mall where you shop, to that after-work beer and a night at the ball game — are likely to be produced by these families and conglomerates."

To get a better feel for the skilful antics involved in this world of high finance, takeovers, mergers, buy-ins and buy-outs, amalgamations, and privatizations, we can refer to the machinations of another powerful family, the Reichmanns, who owned Canada's largest private development company, Olympia and York Developments Ltd. In 1979 Olympia and York went after English Property Corp. Ltd,

Diagram 2.1

The Edward and Peter Bronfman Group
Selected Investments Resource Mining and Development–1996
(Numbers in brackets indicate percentage ownership.)

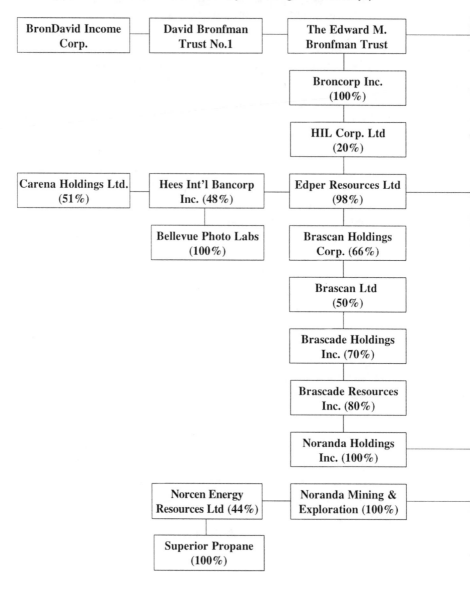

Diagram 2.1 contd.

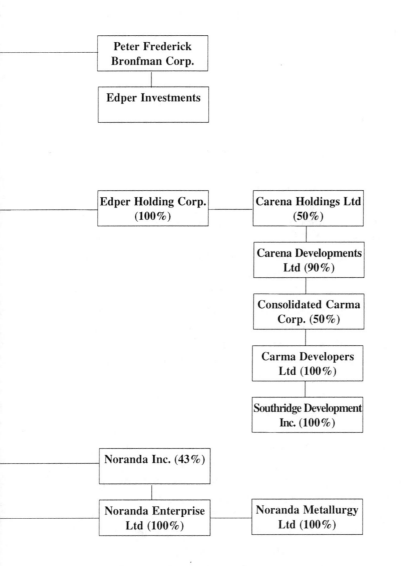

Source: "Intercorporate Ownership–1996" Statistics Canada #61-517-XPB (pp. 5–7).

Britain's third-largest property company, which in turn controlled Trizec Corp., Canada's second-largest public real estate company. At the time Carena-Bancorp, owned by Edward and Peter Bronfman, was part of Trizec and gave the Bronfmans voting control of the latter. In a deal worth over $157 million, the Bronfmans chose not to oppose the takeover bid of English Property by Olympia and York, but they managed to retain management control of Trizec, while agreeing to share ownership of it with the Reichmanns.

The complexities do not end here. There are many levels of decision making within and among subsidiary firms and enterprises: for example, directors, vice presidents, chief executive officers, chairpersons, managers, supervisors. Generally speaking, major decisions relating to the direction of the firm, new initiatives, buying and investing, or selling off of holdings are made by the boards of directors concerned. As we know, however, board members, who can also be owners or shareholders in the company, are appointed by the corporate owners and are directly responsible to them. Board members in turn appoint VPs, CEOs, chairpersons, managers, and other functionaries, and all decisions must reflect the interests of the owners of the parent company at the top.

Capitalist control of the economy is thus maintained via a complex network of overlapping and interlocking directorships on the boards of leading industrial and commercial enterprises, banks, insurance, trust, mortgage, and investment companies, and in other important economic sectors. Over recent decades numerous studies have shown how very little the picture of capitalist ownership and control of major institutions in the Canadian economy has changed. Focusing on concentration of ownership in Canadian-owned corporations, John Porter, author of the well-known book, *The Vertical Mosaic* (1965), found that between 1948 and 1950 some 985 individuals, Canada's economic elite, held directorships in the 170 dominant corporations, banks, and insurance companies in the country. Another study that examined the concentration of economic power in Canada (Ashley 1957) found that in 1955, 97 individuals who held directorships in the Bank of Montreal, the Royal Bank of Canada, the Canadian Bank of Commerce, and the Bank of Nova Scotia, also shared among them 930 directorships in other corporations in other sectors of the economy. Porter's best-known student, Wallace Clement, found similar and increasingly dense patterns of corporate and directorship links among the leading banks and insurance companies,

Diagram 2.2

The Edward and Peter Bronfman Group
Selected Financial Investments–1996
(Numbers in brackets indicate percentage ownership.)

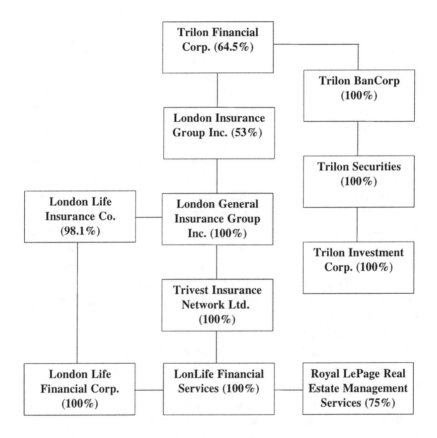

Source: "Intercorporate Ownership–1996" Statistics Canada #61-517-XPB (pp. 5–7).

trust and mortgage companies, utilities, mining, resource, and manufacturing sectors.

In the 1980s, Diane Francis, who focused less on corporate and
directorship links, chose to highlight the leading family dynasties of
Canada and came up with a similarly dismal picture of economic
concentration. In 1986, she began *Controlling Interest: Who Owns
Canada?*, with a quotation from the president of Cadillac Fairview
Corp., who feared that "in a number of years there will be six groups
running this country." She then went on to offer a very pessimistic
economic forecast for Canada, pointing to the existence of 32 parasitic family dynasties more interested in enriching themselves by
taking ever-larger pieces of the Canadian economic pie than in en-
larging that pie for others to share. And they do this with the full
blessing of Parliament and the courts, which understand very little
about economics, and which are consequently powerless to stop their
mergers, takeovers, buy-outs, and assorted other economic machinations. In the process they smother small businesses, chase away new
capital, sacrifice Canadian jobs, and abuse taxpayers who end up
footing the bill for their gambles. Francis commented, "Without
regulation, Canada's corporate barons have played fast and loose
with tax and securities laws, and sometimes their actions have bor-
dered on theft," though arrests and convictions are rare. Thus, as
Forcese pointed out in his 1997 *The Canadian Class Structure*:
"unlike the wage earner, the accumulated wealth of the upper class
is not disclosed, and generally not taxed."

Into the 1990s, when unemployment rose sharply, and when those
still employed had their salaries frozen for three and four years, the
wealthy in Canada continued to enjoy one of the lowest rates of
taxation in the world.

Findings such as these make one gasp at the thinking of most
Canadians, who seem to believe that the shareholders of these large
corporations are numerous and broadly representative of the total
population. Nothing could be further from the truth, but governments
willingly cooperate in such concentration of ownership and perpetuate the popular fiction, because the state in capitalist society has two
principal responsibilities: first, to ensure the long-term reproduction
of capitalism and capitalist institutions and, second, to protect the
interests of the various fractions of the capitalist class. Viewing class
in structural terms, therefore, the very senior levels of government,
including the high-level state bureaucrats such as the prime minister,
the provincial premiers, members of federal and provincial cabinets,

senators, and directors of Crown corporations, should also be seen as part of the capitalist class, because they play such a crucial role in regulating relations between capital and labour, and because they have a clear commitment to the maintenance of capitalism and those who benefit most from it. Because our analysis is focused less on the personalities of these individuals than on the structural positioning among classes in society, it is not difficult to see how the offices occupied by state bureaucrats can cast them in a clearly antagonistic role when dealing with labour. Although these individuals hold political power only temporarily, after they leave office they revert to their socially privileged, bourgeois class pursuits, cancel their blind trusts and re-join at very senior levels the large corporate firms they came from — to carry on business as usual. Their role in the picture of social inequality in Canada is unmistakable.

The Middle Class or Petty Bourgeoisie

The big capitalists might be in a league of their own. There is, however, another class of property owners that cannot be left out of any analysis of social inequality in Canada. This is the middle class, or the petty bourgeoisie. As we will see, when Canadians claim to belong to the middle class, it is in part this large, ill-defined, amorphous group that they have in mind. We say "in part" because there are some strata of the proletariat or working class that shade into the middle class and confuse the picture. This confusion is directly related to the distinction between "class" and "occupation" and feeds into the myth of mobility that the average Canadian employs in his or her denial of entrenched social inequality in the society: "Because working Canadians are a stratified social class, with gradations of income and benefit associated with different jobs, the class character of society is less apparent and certainly not clear-cut" (Forcese 1997:42).

During the period when Marx wrote, the petty bourgeoisie was largely composed of independent commodity producers: farmers, fishermen, artisans, and other class groupings that were characteristic of a feudal-agricultural order. They were distinguished by the fact that they owned their own productive property, usually land and simple agricultural, fishing, or mechanical implements, and subsisted without having either to buy or sell wage labour. Family labour and self-exploitation were central to their economic pursuits.

Marx felt that, faced with the march of industry and the spread of capitalism, this class of independent commodity producers was doomed to disappear. The history of small fishers, farmers, and artisans in Canada partially bears Marx out on this score. In the fishery this is clearly evident as big ships with modern technology and huge capacity are able to process and package their catch while still at sea, not to mention the prohibitive costs associated with helicopters that target schools of fish from the air, Japanese drift-net fishing, and so on. In agriculture, with increased competition from large, mechanized, and capitalized operators, members of this class have lost control of the land and have either converted to wage work on farms now owned by big capital or, more often, moved to urban areas seeking to sell their wage labour. While about 40% of Canada's active labour force was employed on the land at the turn of the century (Johnson 1979:94), by 1995 the figure was only about 3% and agricultural unemployment stood at a mere 0.17%. These statistics show a clear desertion of the agricultural sector by those who had become displaced by large, capital-intensive farm operations (Statistics Canada Cat. 71-201).

Proletarianization is the process whereby a person or population moves from a situation of self-sufficiency in the ownership of the means of production to reliance on wages and employment by others for survival. This process has been constant in the history of all capitalist societies as property ownership has become more concentrated in fewer hands and ever-larger segments of the population have become propertyless.

The pressures placed on the family farm by big banks have been well publicized for many years, and as increasing numbers of them declare bankruptcy the process of proletarianization simply accelerates. In 1984, for example, out of a total agricultural labour force of 491,000 (Statistics Canada Cat. 71-201), 51% were self-employed (Statistics Canada Cat. 71-582). Increasingly, small primary producers, caught in a cost–price squeeze and mortgaged to the hilt, are forced to abandon the family farm or the inshore fishery.

The Canadian petty bourgeoisie has traditionally included two other groups, small, retail business sector and a variety of independent, skilled, and semi-skilled trades. The former is made up of "mom and pop" grocery stores, pet stores, second-hand and repair shops, local restaurants and coffee houses, pawnbrokers, and a host of other small business ventures. Independent entrepreneurs in the latter sector include truckers with their own rigs, taxi drivers who own their own vehicles and plates, carpenters, plumbers, electricians, auto mechanics, barbers and hairdressers, cobblers, tailors, and seamstresses. Very much like the independent commodity producers of this class who fell victim to the corporate capitalist penetration of agriculture and fishing, these two groups are also under severe economic pressure. For example, as the powerful Beckers, Mac's Milk, and 7 Eleven chain stores have all but eliminated the corner grocery store, Canadian Tire, Speedy Muffler, and Quality Lube have come to replace the local auto repair shop. Meanwhile, McDonald's, Wendy's, and Burger King have sounded the death knell of thousands of family-owned restaurants.

The New Middle Class or New Petty Bourgeoisie

As the structure of Canadian society has changed dramatically in the past half century, so too has its middle class. This class has now expanded to incorporate an array of occupations that reflect changing economic realities. Thus, whereas the traditional middle class of farmers, fishers, and artisans were described as "bourgeois" because they owned productive property, they were different from capitalists in that they did not employ or exploit wage labour. The new middle class, on the other hand, is only defined as property owning to the extent that technical skill, specialized knowledge, and professional training are seen as "property" to be bought and sold on the open market. This is where Weber's concern with marketable skills and their role in enhancing life chances comes into the picture. To Weber, one's social class position is conditioned largely by the forces of supply and demand. In the bureaucratic society Weber envisaged, "ownership" of skill and know-how were key determinants of income, power, control, status, and occupational mobility.

Another thing that distinguishes the new middle class is that they are professionals, in the fullest sense of the word. In Marxist terms, they are the "surplus class" of unproductive workers, as opposed to the manual working class that produces the goods and wealth on which the capitalist system actually runs. As business people, middle-range politicians, office managers and assorted white-collar professionals, this large and growing sector comprises the functionaries of capitalism. They help the capitalists make their profits and ensure the continuity of the system. Their jobs are seen as careers, they earn salaries as opposed to wages, and they have a fair measure of personal flexibility in their daily schedules. Given their generally pleasant conditions of work, the great deal of autonomy that comes with their jobs, their tremendous control over the labour (and lives) of others beneath them in the bureaucratic hierarchy, and the fact that their salaries as unproductive workers are higher than the economic contributions they make to the society, members of this new class fraction are neither alienated nor exploited.

The professional sector of the middle class includes highly trained and skilled members of the professions, both self-employed and salaried: doctors, lawyers, architects, engineers, accountants, research scientists, university professors, consultants, and even certain high-profile journalists. As professionals, their power is not derived from personal, material wealth. Rather, it resides in their specialized knowledge and technical expertise, which are in high market demand. They are all certified by institutions of higher learning, hold membership in professional associations, and are usually subject to codes of conduct drawn up by their respective professional communities. It is not unusual for them to earn salaries in the six-figure range and to enjoy lifestyles corresponding to their earning power. They have a large measure of autonomy and flexibility in their jobs, retain control of their working conditions, and are fairly politically conscious of their interests as a group. Through their associations, they are capable of cohesive political action.

There is also a related managerial sector made up of highly paid managers of industrial, commercial, financial, and other related enterprises. Generally sporting MBA, MSc (Management), Certified General Accounting, and law degrees, they usually earn annual salaries running from $70 or $80 thousand to over $200 thousand, live in houses that cost between $350 and $500 thousand, drive cars worth between $60 and $80 thousand, own power boats and yachts valued at over $100 thousand, take frequent luxury vacations, and, in short, lead unbelievably affluent lifestyles.

Very much like their professional counterparts, these people, whose "property" is limited to their managerial skills, specialized knowledge, and administrative know-how, clearly do not belong to the class of rich capitalists. Their power and control of decision making, though by no means negligible, are delegated by others and circumscribed by the company that hires them. It is also unlikely that they can wield enough economic clout and political cohesion as a class fraction to significantly affect the economy at the national or even the provincial level.

Consistent with our use of power and control, whether derived from property or marketable knowledge, as criteria for membership in the new middle class, we can also include middle-range members of government and the civil service: deputy ministers and their appointees, members of Parliament and provincial legislatures, managers and heads of special commissions, judges, and career military and police officers of high rank. While, on one hand, they obviously do not have the same amount of power, status, income, and influence as prime ministers, premiers, cabinet members, and directors of Crown corporations and so do not qualify for membership among the rich capitalists, on the other hand, they are not exactly powerless; indeed, they are far from it.

Marx was correct about the decline of the traditional middle class. But it seems that Weber was more insightful about the new middle class, which is growing quickly at the professional and managerial levels, largely because of the expansion of the welfare state, the wider provision of social services, and the increasing involvement of government in the economy through various marketing boards. As the state bureaucracy expands, the power and control of decision making among this sector of the middle class can also be expected to grow.

Contradictory Class Locations

A considerable amount of interest has been generated about the political inclinations of the new middle class. If they do indeed form a class that is politically conscious, organized, and capable of mobilizing its members in the sense we have been discussing the concept, can we identify what their interests are? Are their interests the same as those of the bourgeoisie? Do all members of the middle class, as owners of small property and holders of a certain degree of power, have a uniform relationship to working-class politics?

These are complex questions for which no simple answers will suffice, but some insight can be gained from Eric Olin Wright, who uses the concepts of "contradiction" and "control" to analyze class relations and politics. Along with the basic antagonisms among classes, Wright noted that some class sectors, particularly those of the new middle class, have stood in a contradictory or confused relation to the larger class structure. By this he meant that the politics of a class sector would be indecisive and reflect the unclear position occupied by that sector in the opposition between capital and labour. For example, using the strict property definition of class, Wright has found that managers, who are non-property owners employed by the capitalist, are by definition proletarian (waged workers). At the same time, their relatively high salaries derived from the exploitation of workers, and their greater autonomy and *control over the means of production*, make them an ally of capital. They thus occupy an ambivalent and contradictory position between the capitalist and working classes. Similarly, factory supervisors, who have only marginally higher incomes than workers, but who also engage in some physical production and have *control of the labour process*, also occupy an ambivalent position between the middle and working classes. Then there is the small employer torn between the middle class and the capitalist class.

The picture became even more complex when Wright distinguished among different degrees of control over investments, the means of production, the labour process, and labour itself. He then introduced the "contradictory class locations" of top managers, middle managers, technocrats, and foremen or line supervisors, all of whom have some degree of control over aspects of these productive resources. Contradictory classes show mixed patterns of control and authority that can easily degenerate into such an array of subclasses that analysis becomes trivial or meaningless. We suggest that, instead of trying to figure out all the combinations and permutations of these contradictory class positions and relationships, it is easier to treat them, not as classes or class sectors, but simply as occupations. In this way, the tensions and antagonisms that can stem from a situation where there are entrenched class inequalities, are ideologically deflected, and social inequalities are cast simply as occupational distinctions. What we are dealing with here is a purportedly open system that offers some mobility within a given class, in this case occupational mobility *within* the middle class, which is widely and erroneously viewed as mobility *between* classes. Where the distinction between class and occupation is not clearly made, people who are occupationally mobile can entertain the fiction that theirs is a classless society or that they all live in the same (middle) class.

Let us now turn our attention to the working class, or proletariat.

The Working Class or Proletariat

Owing to the movement out of the middle class into wage labour and the increasing concentration of property ownership in Canada and other advanced capitalist countries, the working class is the fastest growing and probably the most occupationally heterogeneous of classes. In these countries, people are generally reluctant to declare themselves members of the proletariat. Even the term "proletariat" is avoided, given its Marxist implications of being radical, prone to confrontation, and revolutionary. In its place the label "working

class" is most commonly used, but even here resistance to self-iden-
tification is common, largely because advanced capitalist societies
maintain a clear separation between manual and mental work and
esteem the latter more highly, and also because the terms working
class and lower class (with all their negative connotations) are often
used synonymously. Members of the working class reluctant to identify themselves as such are also by and large the most likely to claim
that they are middle class, or that Canada is a classless society.

This notwithstanding, the proletariat, or working class, is an empirical reality, and it is the largest of all classes. In Canada, the 1991
census lists a total population of 27,296,859 (Statistics Canada Cat.
93-304 p.13). Out of an economically active labour force of
14,474,945, the census lists 13,005,505, or 90% as having worked
for wages (Statistics Canada, Cat. 93-324 p.110; Cat. 93-326 p.2).
But as we have discussed, working for a wage or a salary is only one
insufficient element in the definition of class. To use a definition
simply tied to ownership of productive property yields a mere two-
class view of society, failing to take into account occupational and
other distinctions within a given class. The working class in Canada
is quite differentiated, running the gamut from semi-professional and
technical workers at the top to agricultural or farm workers at the
bottom. Among semi-professionals are those who possess some cultural capital, limited amounts of power, and a restricted measure of
control over others, even though they do not own property. At the
other end of the spectrum are farm workers, who in 1991 were the
worst paid workers in Canada (Statistics Canada Cat. 93-332).

Following the categories developed by Statistics Canada to describe the working class, we can speak of five broad occupational
groupings within it. First are the semi-professional and technical
workers who make decent wages and salaries and who, even if their
jobs do not necessarily require it, might also hold a college degree
or diploma. This group includes a wide variety of occupations such
as teachers, social workers, x-ray and dental technicians, computer
operators, engineering assistants, nurses, master mechanics, and li-
brarians. Also included are those in the leisure and entertainment
industry, such as scriptwriters, performers and musicians, artists, and
certain media people like news writers and reporters. In the minds
of the average Canadian, this semi-professional and technical sector
of the working class is often confused with the middle class, and this
contributes to the belief that we all live in one, big middle-class
society.

People in these occupations are usually quite visible in the working-class community. They are white-collar employees who generally enjoy quite pleasant working conditions, earn a comfortable living, can accumulate various material possessions, and, as we have said, can often boast some post-secondary education. Because of this they are given a certain community status and often delude themselves into thinking they are part of a mobile segment in a fluid middle-class society. At the same time, other segments of the working class view them as models that are not only deserving of emulation, but are also within their own reach. The ideological implications of all this are very real, especially given the heavy traffic between this upper rung of the working-class ladder and the lower rungs of the middle-class ladder. Many of these people have parents in lower sectors of the working class, so, given semi-professionals' relatively higher wages and good working conditions, the upward move is a sign of intergenerational upward mobility. Ironically, however, for some, "semi-professional" means a drop in class status. Some of the children, usually daughters, of middle-class parents enter this sector after college.

The second grouping within the working class is made up of white-collar and other workers in offices, stores, supermarkets, and even on the street. This is the very diverse clerical and sales sector of the working class. Among the clerical occupations are such office personnel as secretaries and stenographers, typists, bookkeepers and accounting clerks, cashiers and tellers, shipping and receiving clerks, receptionists and information clerks, mail and postal workers, telephone operators, and messengers. In the sales sector there are general sales clerks, door-to-door salespersons, service station attendants, insurance, real estate, and advertising sales personnel, and telemarketers. Traditionally, a high school diploma was sufficient for entry to this sector, but as the economy has contracted over the past two decades it is not uncommon to find college graduates doing these jobs for very low pay (see Table 2.3).

A third category lumps a wide array of working-class occupations and income groups under the rubric of "service workers." Statistics Canada reported that two out of every three Canadian workers in 1991 were found in service producing industries. (Cat. 93-326 p.1). Service workers are found in restaurants and fast food outlets, theatres and cinemas, hotels, and protective services. Some common, poorly paid occupations in this sector include chefs and cooks, ushers, waiters and bartenders, cleaners, baggage handlers, and train

Table 2.3

Selected Occupations by Average 1990 Income and Number

Census category	Job title	Income ($)	Number
Health & Medicine	Physicians & surgeons	83,407	85,635
	Dentists	95,728	54,700
	Veterinarians	86,623	13,025
Managerial & administrative	Senior government managers	63,870	157,065
	Engineering & architectural managers	60,611	16,430
	Construction managers	52,878	32,035
	Sales and marketing managers	59,625	4,925
Clerical	Bookkeepers	20,000	410,685
	Cashiers & tellers	9,543	358,695
	Data processing	20,019	141,000
	Stock clerks	17,807	115,110
	File clerks	13,982	40,520
	Phone operators	17,729	31,050
Sales	Wholesale & retail	16,023	739,285
	Door-to-door	13,581	15,370
	Real estate	35,128	83,170
	Insurance	32,590	65,345
Service	Chefs & cooks	11,718	229,925
	Bartenders	10,681	41,590
	Food & beverage servers	7,265	308,995
Farming/Fishing	Livestock handlers	11,869	34,205
	Crop hands	9,169	47,095
	Nursery attendants	12,210	99,430
	Trapping	7,020	1,045
	Fishing	12,835	6,470
Forestry	Forestry & logging	10,360	18,070

Source: adapted from Statistics Canada (Cat. 93-332). 1991 Census.

porters. Among the better paid are armed forces personnel, fire fighters and police officers, prison guards, and certain security personnel.

The fourth category includes manual production workers, the traditional blue-collar workers or industrial proletariat employed at the industrial sites, in the factories, mines, and warehouses of the capitalists. Counted among their numbers are craftworkers (machinists, linemen, crane operators, die makers), transport operatives (railway workers, truck drivers, forklift operators), machine operatives (assemblers, cutters, fitters, welders, punch press operators), labourers (longshoremen, warehousers, stevedores), and construction workers. As is well known, these jobs are physically very demanding, repetitious, and unimaginative, and with increasing mechanization and computerization of blue-collar operations, many are subject to "deskilling." Consequently, many workers in this category suffer high levels of alienation and exploitation at the hands of supervisors and foremen, who are themselves pressured from above by their superiors. Although the average wages of these workers might compare well with some other categories, long hours and overtime, frequent job-related accidents, unpleasant conditions, abusive supervisors, and general occupational insecurity are just some of the adversities they have to contend with on a routine basis. These workers are very productive relative to many other sectors, and on their backs much of Canada's economic prosperity rests.

The fifth and final category of the working class is made up of the most powerless and miserably paid workers, who engage in farming, as well as the specialized activities of stock raising, dairy production, logging, and even fishing. Specific occupational designations in this sector include general farm workers, livestock and crop farm workers, horticultural and animal husbandry occupations, harvesting labourers, and nursery and greenhouse workers. As can be seen in Table 2.3, wages of workers in this sector are the lowest in Canada and in no way reflect or acknowledge the vital contributions that these workers make to the daily survival of every Canadian.

Compared with the rich lifestyles of the high-flying Canadian Establishment, members of the working class live an entirely different reality. Even if we were to leave the Canadian Establishment out of the picture (since technically speaking they tend not to have "occupations"), the disparities are staggering. According to Statistics Canada, the average income for the 10 highest-paid middle-class occupations in 1990 was $73,313, five times more than the average for the 10 lowest-paid occupations, which stood at $15,092 (Statistics

Canada, Cat. 93-332 p.2). The former category includes judges, magistrates, physicians, surgeons, dentists, pilots, and university professors, while the latter covers such occupations as textile fabrication, apparel and furnishing service, chefs and cooks, sewing machine operators, farm workers, waiters, and cleaners. There are many, many more cooks, cleaners, and farm workers than there are judges, physicians, pilots, and so on.

Further, while the figure for the top 10 might appear to be low, it must be borne in mind that we are dealing here with *averages*. Newcomers to the professions, such as assistant professors and recently graduated doctors or lawyers not in private practice, lower the average considerably. But this is only a temporary condition in professions where there are no ceilings on incomes. At the other extreme, among the bottom 10, where entry-level incomes will also distort the overall average, the range of incomes is not all that great, and most occupations have ceilings. Add to this the fact that the wealthy tend to be more healthy, to have longer life expectancy, to enjoy better life chances, to be more physically secure, and to be better able to protect themselves legally and otherwise, and entirely new dimensions of social inequality begin to become apparent.

The worlds of these two classes may seem to be different. Nevertheless, they are part of the same Canada. Those in the menial, dead-end, dirty, low-paying occupations simply represent the flip side of wealth, privilege, and power in our supposedly classless society. Yet this does not come close to completing the picture of social inequality in the country. For there is yet another world out there: the world of the poor.

The Poor

> Poverty might merit pity but not provoke indignation. The poor exist because of the rules of the game or the ill-fortune of destiny. Until 20 or 30 years ago, poverty was the fruit of injustice ... much has changed in a short time. Now poverty is unconnected to injustice, and the very notion of injustice has been effaced and nearly disappeared. The moral code at the end of the century does not condemn injustice, only failure. (Galeano, no date)

Consistent with the generally rosy image Canadians have of themselves and their society, we also tend to deny the existence of poverty, or we explain it away as the result of individual laziness and

Table 2.4

Quintile Shares of Total (100%) Income
in 1981, 1986, and 1991

	Families			Unattached individuals			All households		
	1981	1986	1991	1981	1986	1991	1981	1986	1991
1st	6.5	6.4	6.4	5.0	5.2	5.4	4.6	4.7	4.7
2nd	12.8	12.4	12.2	9.5	10.4	10.6	10.9	10.4	10.3
3rd	18.3	17.9	17.6	15.7	15.3	15.6	17.6	17.0	16.6
4th	24.1	24.0	23.9	25.1	24.4	24.7	25.2	24.9	24.7
Top	38.3	39.3	39.9	44.7	44.7	43.7	41.7	43.1	43.8

Source: Ross et al., *The Canadian Fact Book on Poverty* (1994:89).

Note: "Total income" refers to all sources of income including government transfers, before taxes. Over the years the distrubution has remained remarkably stable indicating a freezing of the inequality patterns in the three categories listed in the table.

personal choice. Writing for the right-wing Fraser Institute in 1992, for example, Christopher Sarlo asserted that "poverty, as it has been traditionally understood, has been virtually eliminated. It is simply not a major problem in Canada" (Sarlo 1992:2). Sarlo's writing typifies the economic and political ideology of the Fraser Institute, the well-known right-wing think tank located in Vancouver, B.C. It extols the virtues of free enterprise capitalism, casts the individual as the sole architect of his or her own destiny, and denies that social processes can be structured into the society. And in one regard this makes sense, for as the noted French sociologist André Béteille says: "poverty is a source of social opprobrium; to be poor in an affluent society is to show a lack of worth" (1969:369).

Thus, declaring that "I am not at all offended by inequality[;] I have no problem with large variations in income and wealth," Sarlo prepared the ground for a conservative defence of the status quo. Because poverty does not exist and inequality is not offensive to him, what is left to conclude? His position fits well with the functionalist treatment of inequality discussed in Chapter 1, in which inequalities in income and wealth are deemed *necessary* and *desirable*, even *innate*. Echoing these precise sentiments, Sarlo continued: "States of well-being or 'ill-being' are essentially *personal* and depend on the *individual's preferences*, expectations and self-image — characteristics which are in turn determined by some *mysterious* mix of biology and environment" (emphasis added). He went on to argue that "poverty is an eminently subjective state" and to make a distinction between "voluntary and involuntary poverty." His clear implication is that in a free society such as Canada's, where good things abound, anyone who is poor chooses this condition deliberately. But because poverty is associated with great physical discomfort, hunger, ill-health, social scorn, loss of self-respect and human dignity, why would anyone want to be poor and pay these severe penalties? Clearly Sarlo's treatment of poverty is very narrowly ideological.

Functionalists insist, however, that in order to motivate the less equal to better themselves, to ensure that the important jobs are filled by the most qualified persons, and to convince the "naturally" talented members of society that they will be well rewarded for their efforts, social inequalities must be preserved. Any attempt by government (or others) to get rid of inequality is doomed to failure because, despite massive government spending on a variety of educational, welfare, and other anti-poverty programs in the past, "The distribution of income is as unequal as it ever was. It is almost as if there were something inevitable or *inherent* about this distribution," as Sarlo puts it (emphasis added). And so Sarlo is confident that "there is nothing intrinsically unjust about inequality in general and the current quintile distributions of income in Canada in particular," even if the top 20% of Canadian households receive about nine times the income of the bottom 20%, or more than the bottom three quintiles combined.

Defining Poverty

Those concerned with the problem of poverty in Canada engage in a great deal of debate over how it should be defined. Much of the debate is carried on between those who prefer to deny or minimize its existence and those who acknowledge it and want to eliminate it. Currently, as part of the general denial of the problem at the government level, there is no *official* measure of poverty in Canada, although several organizations have addressed it in one way or another, including: Statistics Canada; Canadian Council on Social Development (CCSD); Senate Special Committee on Poverty; Metropolitan Toronto Social Planning Council; Montreal Diet Dispensary [Guidelines]; Fraser Institute [Poverty Lines].

Table 2.5

Lines of Income Inequality Developed by the CCSD in 1994

Family size (no. of persons)	Income level ($)
1	13,770
2	22,950
3	27,540
4	32,130
5	36,720
6	41,310
7	45,900

Source: Ross et al., *The Canadian Fact Book on Poverty* (1994: 16).

All of the above organizations differ on what exact measures should be employed in the definition of poverty, but, with the exception of the Fraser Institute, they all agree that poverty really exists and that it poses a serious problem for the whole society. One important aspect of their disagreement involves differences between absolute and relative concepts of poverty.

Absolute poverty is linked to the cost of a basic "basket" of essential goods and services, which is assigned a fixed dollar amount. In its strictest sense, it assumes the barest of circumstances and envisages the poor eating at soup kitchens, getting some groceries from food banks, living in community shelters or even on the street, buying second-hand clothing, and having no leisure or recreation. Given such a definition, an annual income of around $2,000 per person would be enough to afford the poor a rock-bottom level of physical existence, and statistically speaking, it would all but remove poverty from the books in Canada. But as a solution to the problem, whether theoretically or statistically, this definition of absolute poverty is clearly unsatisfactory and unrealistic, as denial always is.

Using figures from Campaign 2000's *Countdown 93* report and data from a House of Commons sub-committee report, *Towards 2000: Eliminating Child Poverty*, the CCSD has come up with a daily dollar figure of $14.60 per person, or $21,300 annually for a family of four, as a bare-bones minimum for survival in 1994. This figure was broken down as follows: for food they used Agriculture Canada's "Thrifty Nutritious Food Plan" as a guide to come up with a daily figure of $4.75, to which they added a daily shelter cost of $7.16 computed from Canada Mortgage and Housing Corporation data. Finally, they factored in the Montreal Diet Dispensary's estimate of $1.22 per day for clothing, and then concluded that "out of the remaining $1.47 per person per day, families need to pay for personal care items, household needs, furniture, telephone, transportation, school supplies, health care and so on." Other costs associated with things such as entertainment, insurance, and religious donations are not included.

In place of any absolute definition of poverty, we prefer a relative approach. Given the vast differences among nations or even among regions of Canada, it is clear that poverty levels and tolerable standards vary greatly from place to place so any meaningful assessment of poverty would have to take as its point of departure the social conditions prevailing at a given time and in a given place. Poverty is therefore *relative*, and cannot simply be tied to subsistence. Human beings are social and must be judged by relevant social comparisons, not by some statistical or absolute imperative that ignores concerns for human decency and dignity. As economist John Kenneth Galbraith wrote about 40 years ago: "People are poverty-stricken when their income, even if adequate for survival, falls markedly behind that of the community. Then they cannot have what the larger community regards as the minimum necessary for decency; and they cannot escape therefore the judgement of the larger community that they are indecent" (1958:323–4). Even if the poor in Canada might be considered comfortable by the standards of another country, the fact remains that they live in Canada, and so must be seen relative to other Canadians.

The CCSD adopts a relative measure of poverty that is both sensible and straightfoward. Focusing on family size and income (see Table 2.5), it uses information from Statistics Canada to establish that the average size of the Canadian family is 3.15 persons and that the average annual income for a family of that size in 1992 was $53,676. It then puts the poverty line at half the average income for the community in question (Canada as a whole or a given province) and factors in adjusted increments for each additional family member. According to CCSD calculations, the rate of household poverty in Canada between 1973 and 1991 stood fairly steady at 20.6%. This means that a little more than one in every five Canadian households is poor. The CCSD adds, however, "when this figure is combined with Canada's population growth over the same period, it translates into an increase of 741,000 poor households."

The foregoing notwithstanding, the fact that the government of Canada seems to prefer the Fraser Institute's absolute approach to poverty over the CCSD's relative one is a cause for concern. As the CCSD's 1994 *Canadian Fact Book on Poverty* clearly demonstrates, the 1992 income of poor households fell well below figures commonly recommended by relative measures. As one example, its authors noted that the income of $8,274 for the average Canadian poor family in 1992 falls $7,376 below the widely recognized low-income line established by Statistics Canada for a lone-parent mother (Ross et al. 1994:5).

What Being Poor Means

There are over two million poor households in Canada. Those hardest hit by the curse of poverty are the young, the elderly, Aboriginals, visible minorities, and women. What is worse, poverty is a vicious circle from which few people ever escape on their own.

Poor people are generally at greater risk of random violence than better-off Canadians. They also tend to be sick more often, receive lower quality medical care, and take longer to recover than non-poor Canadians. And so they miss school and work more often. Compared with more comfortably placed members of society, they are less likely to do well at school, less likely to have good jobs, and less likely to feel optimistic about their long-term chances of success. At the same time, they are more likely to experience the whole range of domestic difficulties that stem from tough economic circumstances — alcoholism and drug addiction, domestic violence, separation and divorce, unwanted pregnancies, and so on — more likely to have problems with the law, and more likely to face discrimination and disrespect from employers, teachers, police officers, politicians, and other authority figures.

Conclusion

Poverty in Canada exists in a social system where government bails out and gives massive subsidies to big businesses, creates tax loopholes for the wealthy, grants tax holidays and other incentives to foreign investors, yet it claims to cherish the ideals of equality and freedom. The contradictions are unmistakable. Canada's poor — the homeless "bag ladies," the mentally ill who roam the streets of our largest cities, the Native people on reserves, poor people within the prison population, struggling single mothers, the unemployed and the underemployed — are eloquent testimony to an unequal social order that is not quite capable of dealing with all the human by-products of capitalism.

The need for social order within an unequal system requires that there be social control. This is where the dominant ideologies of liberalism, individualism, and free enterprise play a central part. Because these ideologies have been promoted so effectively, most Canadians believe that hard work, individual initiative, and a measure of good luck are key ingredients of success. Those who call the shots in Canada, as in all capitalist societies, have to find ways of instilling such ideological mind-sets among the least advantaged while continuing to preserve economic and political competition, which takes place largely among members of the privileged classes. But some amount of social welfare must also be available for the social reproduction of those who are "less equal," and on whose labour power the system relies. Class inequality is the most fundamental (though not the only) form of inequality in capitalist society.

3

Race, Racial Inequality, and Resistance

Much has been written on the *economic* consequences of racial and ethnic stratification for those on the receiving end of discriminatory practices in Canada: poor life chances, low-paying and menial jobs, higher levels of unemployment, substandard housing, ill health, higher rates of criminal conviction, and so on. Less well documented, however, are some of the *political* consequences of such stratification. How do the victims of prejudice and discrimination react on a daily basis to the more or less constant attempts to devalue them? What strategies do they use to cope with challenges to their political and human rights? Without wishing to minimize the economic costs of prejudice and discrimination, it is political questions such as these that will constitute the main focus of this chapter.

The great social diversity that characterizes Canada today is enhanced by a rich and complex ethno-cultural mix. Canada is touted as a country of immigrants, and it is only to be expected that the contemporary Canadian social fabric would reflect the baggage of its different peoples: when they arrived, their numerical strength, and their subsequent contribution to the composition of Canadian society. Canadian society and culture, however, have a unique reality that cannot be reduced to the various indigenous, European, Asian, African, and American elements that comprise it. Over time all of these elements have become uniquely fused into a national culture. But Canada is also a vast country with diverse regional identities, so one must always be cautious when generalizing about "Canadian culture."

As a lived process, Canada's national culture embodies the historical record of ethnic encounters, the cooperation, competition, and conflict that marked those encounters, and the ongoing power struggles that define contemporary politics, economics, and cultural production. It is in this context that we seek to understand the

Table 3.1

Ethnic Composition of Canada's Population in 1991

Aboriginal	5.6
British only	28.1
French only	22.8
British and/or French and Other	14.2
British and French	4.0
Caribbean, Latin-, Central-, South American	2.2
Black	2.7
Canadian	9.2
Asian/Arab/African	19.6
All European	49.7

Source: *Canadian Social Trends*, No. 3 (1993: 20).

ethno-racial forces at play in Canadian society. We describe the Canadian economy and society as capitalist, based fundamentally on class exploitation and the pursuit of profit; the sectors of the capitalist class that dominate the state are able to use a variety of means to further their interests.

Racialization

Among the more successful strategies employed to distract and divide the working classes is the development of the ideology of "race," which holds that the human population can be divided into discrete biological races, each with a set of accompanying genetic, intellectual, moral and behavioural predispositions. Some races are thus socially constructed as superior and others as inferior. This is the process of *racialization*, whereby the wider population comes to view a given group stereotypically. Racialization applies particularly to those who are negatively constructed by authorities such as the police and the courts, and by those who control key institutions, such as the educational system and the media. Racialization increases class exploitation and erodes economic well-being. By providing the social basis for categorizing a sector of the labour force as inferior, it provides the specific justification for lowering wages in that sector, and encourages a lowering of wages across the board.

Throughout the recent history of colonialism and imperialism, various classes, and sometimes whole populations, have been racialized. One well-known example is the indigenous inhabitants of North America, who survived almost total annihilation only to find themselves confined to reservations that make up only a fraction of their ancestral lands. Indeed, the 1989 *Annual Report of the Canadian Human Rights Commissioner* noted, "If there is any single issue on which Canada cannot hold its head high in the international community, any single area in which we can be accused of falling down on our obligations, it is in the area of aboriginal relations" (quoted in Elliott and Fleras 1992:160;164).

From the outset of colonial rule, while their lands were being stolen and their cultures plundered, the peoples of Canada's First Nations were stigmatized as godless, scalp-hunting, savage, hostile, "red men," not to be trusted. After some 400 years, such intense racialization has produced a population with infant mortality rates 60% higher than the national average, death rates that are four times the national average, and suicide rates among young people six times the national average. Regionally, for example, while Natives comprise 12% of the Prairie population, they represent 40% of inmates in Prairie prisons. The 1991 census shows Aboriginal males as ranking twentieth in income out of twenty-one ethnic groups listed. Add to this the fact that unemployment for Natives ranges between 35% and 75%, and where they are employed, it tends to be in low-status jobs categorized as "other": fishing, trapping, and logging. Finally, on such dimensions as education, health, and housing, Natives are consistently at the bottom of the social ladder, which spells disaster for them as a group.

These are the unmistakable effects of racialization and racism practised over the years against Canada's First Nations. The key point is that race is a social, not a biological construct. Race is a construct that has been used by the dominant classes to promote their interests throughout history from slavery and colonialism right up to the present day. But just as the dominant classes can actively pursue their interests, so too can the dominated classes. And though the latter may lack the same access to power, they still can and do offer different forms of resistance to their domination. This said, it is also important to emphasize that those who might offer resistance do not necessarily have a critical understanding of the sources of racism,

Table 3.2

Male Education, Occupation, and Income by Ethnic Group in 1981 and 1991

Ethnic groups	Years of education (mean)	White-collar jobs (%)	Income 1981 (male mean age 20–60)	Income 1991 (male mean age 20–60)
Non-visible minority				
Jewish	14.7	56.4	$19,054	$37,146
British	14.0	42.7	$17,360	$29,928
French	13.5	41.7	$15,776	$27,222
Dutch	12.4	31.5	$16,461	$30,888
German	12.4	28.9	$16,887	$31,506
Ukrainian	11.1	19.0	$17,109	$34,110
Italian	9.0	15.2	$15,588	$29,550
Portuguese	7.9	7.7	$14,776	$26,926
Visible minority				
West Asian and Arab	14.2	43.2	——	$21,284
South Asian	14.2	36.4	——	$25,718
Chinese	14.9	34.3	$14,120	$26,392
Southeast Asian	13.4	29.0	——	$24,080
Black and Caribbean	13.3	22.9	$14,442	$23,346

Note: The category of white-collar occupations includes managerial and administrative, natural science, engineering, mathematics, social sciences, teaching, medicine and health, and artistic, literary, and related occupations. As is obvious, however, the above "income means" include all categories of occupations.

Source: Driedger (1996:199;247).

Table 3.3

Rate of Participation of Visible Minorities and Other Canadians in the Economy in 1991

Visible minorities	%	Managers	Professionals
Chinese	26	9	15
South Asians	20	8	13
Blacks	20	7	13
West Asians and Arabs	11	12	15
Filipinos	7	3	12
Latin Americans	5	5	8
Southeast Asians	5	4	10
Japanese	3	13	19
Koreans	2	17	10
Pacific Islanders	0.2	5	9
Other Canadians	10	13	13

nor have they necessarily developed an alternative vision of their society. Thus, their resistance must not automatically be presumed to be carefully tailored to address or eliminate the practice of racism.

In this chapter, therefore, we will take for granted that the development of capitalism in Canada paralleled the development of what is called "a country of immigrants." We also assume that the arrival of different immigrant groups influenced, and was influenced by, the dialectical tensions between capital and labour, and that in the process, some groups were racialized by others. Viewed in this way, the unequal rankings of ethnic groups in Canada by income and other material measures (see Table 3.2) are fundamentally social in origin. They are firmly tied to the wider class and economic structures of our society.

Table 3.3 (contd.)

Manual work	Service workers	Labour force participation	Unemploy-ment rate (%)
13	15	63	10
19	9	69	16
16	13	69	15
10	11	63	16
14	25	75	8
29	13	61	19
32	11	60	17
8	9	66	6
8	8	66	8
15	14	69	7
13	10	68	10

Source: *Canadian Social Trends*, No. 37, Summer (1995:2–8).

Depending on historical circumstances, place of origin, culture, and "typical" physical appearance, some immigrant groups are generally able by the second or third generations to transcend racialization and normalize their terms of participation in Canada's economy and society, whether as capitalists, independent professionals, or workers. These are, generally speaking, "white" immigrants from Britain, western, eastern, and southern Europe, and from the United States. Immigrant groups from such areas as Africa, India, Asia, and the Caribbean, however, Canada's so-called visible minorities, have found it more difficult to escape racial definition and stereotyping, and they are less likely to be represented among the country's elite. They are, however, highly visible in a wide variety of low-paying, menial, and working-class occupations, where rates of exploitation and alienation are usually excessive, and where incidents of racism are commonplace.

Visible Minorities

Following passage of the federal Employment Equity Act in 1986, four groups were designated as "high priority" for receiving special attention in hiring decisions: women, Aboriginals, persons with disabilities, and members of visible minorities. Within the latter group, overwhelmingly made up of immigrants, 10 specific sub-groups have been differentiated for census and other governmental purposes: blacks, Chinese, Filipinos, Japanese, Koreans, Latin Americans, Other Pacific Islanders, South Asians, Southeast Asians and West Asians, and Arabs. Canada's visible minorities are made up of a vast array of different types of people. Japanese and Chinese, for example, though seen as minorities are viewed and treated very differently from blacks and Latin Americans. The former have widely differing levels of education, self-employment, and general involvement in the labour force than the latter groups. They also have widely varying types of family structures and other such forms of community support that are so crucial to the success of any immigrant group in a prejudiced society.

Nevertheless, taken as a whole, visible minorities in Canada have more difficulty than others in securing employment. And as non-European immigration has risen, so too have incidents of prejudice and discrimination.

Recent human rights cases suggest that entrenched prejudices and discriminatory practices hinder the promotion of visible minorities to managerial positions in the federal civil service. Visible minorities are clearly separated from the rest of Canadian society by income. Even when a visible minority member is better educated than another person, this does not mean that she or he will enjoy a comparably higher income.

Visible minorities must devise coping mechanisms for dealing with their daily engagements with the wider society. They must resist society's racism and the constant attempts to consign them to racial categories. But before discussing those forms of resistance, it will be useful to briefly put the historical evolution of Canada's ethno-racial and ethno-cultural fabric into context.

Table 3.4

Education and Occupational Attainment of Visible Minorities and Other Canadians in 1991

Population aged 25–44	University education (%)	Less than high school (%)	Professionals (%)	Managers (%)
Visible minorities	25	33	39	13
Other Canadians	17	39	52	18

Source: *Canadian Social Trends.* No. 37 (1995:8).

Historical Context

The constitutional definition of Canada betrays an entrenched racism against the original inhabitants of this vast land. When Canadians speak of the country's "founding groups," for example, they refer exclusively to the French and British who arrived as colonizers and exploiters in the sixteenth and seventeenth centuries. Those who were colonized, exploited, and decimated, the first Canadians, are not mentioned. Right up to the 1960s, when politicians wrestled with the definition of the country's cultural identity, Canada's First Nations were still excluded: the 1963 *Report of the Royal Commission on Bilingualism and Biculturalism* made no concessions to Indian languages or cultures. The two languages and cultures intended in the title of that report were French and English, giving the clear indication that other ethnic groups, who were either here before the arrival of the French and British, or who came subsequently, were of lesser importance.

Between the mid-sixteenth and early seventeenth centuries, when Jacques Cartier, Samuel de Champlain and others were establishing the first French settlements in New France, they encountered a variety of Indian peoples and cultures. Among them were the Iroquois, the Huron, and the Algonquin, who offered differing degrees of cooperation with, and resistance to, the European intruders, and also to one another. In time, when the French came to realize that they would not find quick riches in the form of precious metals (as the

Spaniards had done in Mexico and Peru), they swiftly turned their attention to the furs the Indians transported to, and traded at, various trading posts. By the middle of the seventeenth century, this fur trade culminated in an alliance between the French, on the one hand, and the Huron and Algonquin, on the other, who supplied furs from the interior. The Iroquois, however, were sworn enemies of the Huron, and they were bent on expelling the French from their land.

When the British moved north and arrived on the scene in the mid-1700s, they encountered a well-developed French fur trading system based in the St. Lawrence Valley and reaching all the way north to Hudson Bay and south to the Gulf of Mexico. Mirroring the wider European hostilities, conflict was as immediate as it was certain. The English befriended the Iroquois and under the royal monopoly charter of the Hudson's Bay Company, they proceeded to penetrate the most lucrative sources of French fur in the northwest. They finally defeated the French in 1759 on the Plains of Abraham, and New France was surrendered to Great Britain.

In the ensuing period, as the British established their political and cultural hegemony over the continent, class interests were unmistakably wrapped up with British, French, and multiple Indian ethno-cultural differences. Realizing the great difficulty involved in completely assimilating Catholic Quebec, several British governors ignored instructions to anglicize the province and opted instead to cultivate the class loyalty of the seigneurs (large landowners), the upper levels of the Catholic clergy, and a powerful lobby of lawyers. Thus, the Quebec Act of 1774 was passed, permitting Catholics to sit on provincial councils, allowing the use of French civil law for commercial and domestic purposes, and legitimizing the seigneurial landowning system.

Britain was at this time keen on thwarting the ambitions for independence of its thirteen American colonies. To this end, the English-speaking, Anglican British made many overtures to the French-speaking, Roman Catholic settlers — *les habitants* — with a view to containing the rebellious Americans. Indeed, one of the precipitating factors in the outbreak of the American Revolution had to do precisely with the Quebec Act, which enlarged Quebec to include much of the Ohio Valley, thus imposing a check on the westward expansion of the thirteen seaboard colonies. When the 1783 Treaty of Paris formally ended the American Revolution, one of its central provisions was the severance of the Ohio country from Quebec and its surrender to the new American republic.

For the next 30 years or so the French and English in Lower and Upper Canada continued to struggle for their respective "rights" to impose their linguistic and cultural identities over the territory under their control. Although the English were clearly in the ascendancy, the French never relinquished the idea of a Catholic, French-speaking Quebec. In the meantime, the Americans, who were never comfortable with British dominance of their ill-defined northern neighbour, hoped to capitalize on the historic French–English animosities and continued to entertain thoughts of ousting the British entirely from the continent. To this end, the leaders of the new American nation encouraged the republican sentiments among the population of Lower Canada. They attempted to play off these sentiments, popularized by the American and French revolutions, against the monarchist leanings of the British Loyalists in Upper Canada. Matters came to a head in the War of 1812. The war accomplished nothing in terms of territory, but it heightened Canadian suspicions of American expansionism and strengthened loyalist sentiments among English Canadians.

In the years following the War of 1812 both Lower and Upper Canada experienced much internal political unrest. The French of Lower Canada feared that moves to unify the country would smother them culturally in the face of the numerically, economically, and militarily superior British; meanwhile the English of Upper Canada were discontented over taxes and customs revenues that seemed to benefit Lower Canada disproportionately. As well, the populations of both provinces embraced liberal and radical politics and opposed the traditional privileges of their respective elite classes. Thus, when economic depression struck in 1837, spontaneous rebellions broke out in both colonies. They were quelled only when Britain sent Lord Durham to investigate as high commissioner and governor general of British North America. In his report, Durham noted that when he arrived: "I expected to find a contest between a government and a people: I found two nations warring in the bosom of a single state: I found a struggle not of principles but of races."

Based on the *Durham Report*, which was decidedly pro-British and spoke of the "superior knowledge, energy, enterprise, and wealth of the English race" the 1840 Act of Union was passed and legally unified Upper and Lower Canada into a single entity.

Rivalry between French- and English-speaking Canadians has persisted and threatens to divide the country. Along with these traditional divides, twentieth-century migrations to Canada have conditioned the development of an ethno-culturally diverse society in which racism is alive and well, and where minorities resist that racism in many different ways. We will consider some of the strategies for resisting racism that different minority groups in contemporary Canadian society have adopted. But, we want to stress the fact that most social conflicts based on race, tribe, ethnicity, or nation are most fruitfully understood as rooted in the class or politico-economic pursuits of elites and those classes that oppose them.

Race, Racism, Ethnicity, and Resistance: Definitions

Race

The first step in defining race is to separate biological from social definitions. In biological terms, race refers to the categorization of people on the basis of certain hereditary characteristics, such as blood type, genetic make-up, and physical appearance. Because a person from one genetic group can interbreed with a person from another genetic group, such categorizations, and combinations of them, offer infinite possibilities.

Some sociobiologists argue that biological differences can explain social differences or social inequalities (Herrnstein and Murray 1994; Rushton 1995). But, such approaches confuse the biological conception of race with its social definition: races are socially imagined categories, and are not biologically real. Above all else, race is fundamentally a political concept. For example, under South Africa's apartheid system, Japanese people were defined as honorary whites for economic reasons, while those of Chinese descent were not. Similarly, the "law of one drop" in the United States, whereby one drop of "black blood" renders a person wholly black, has enabled all kinds of convenient race switching. Where did the idea of skin colour as a basis for differentiating among the races arise? Why not use blood type, hair colour, or ear size?

According to Robert Miles, "If 'races' are not naturally occurring populations, the reasons and conditions for the social processes whereby the discourse of 'race' is employed in an attempt to label, constitute and exclude social collectivities should be the focus of attention rather than be assumed to be a natural and universal process" (1989:73).

The politics of race begins where the biological and social conceptions of race intersect. As long as there are those who want to justify social practices by resorting to biological claims, disagreement and conflict will be the norm. In other words, when jobs, housing, education, credit, and other social amenities are distributed along racial (biological) lines, people are unlikely to agree on who gets what. Those who perceive the system of allocation to be unfair will usually find ways of resisting or protesting.

Concern with race, then, is ideological and serves the structure of class dominance wherever it is invoked. Those who insist that races are real will usually have a political agenda according to which social contrivances such as poverty, intelligence, powerlessness, or even class privilege are cast as *natural*. Thus they seek entirely to remove responsibility for these social contrivances from the realm of social interaction. No one is to blame. Acceptance of the term "race" legitimizes it, enabling such talk as "whites are *naturally* smarter than blacks." This attempts to legitimize a socially produced situation by giving it the veneer of a natural, biological, inflexible fact.

Few serious scientists continue to give the term "race" any credibility. This does not mean, however, that there can be no common-sense understandings and uses of it. As Miles noted, "The fact that the idea of 'race' continues to be employed in commonsense testifies to its continuing practical rather than scientific utility." This is where the concern with racism becomes relevant. Because so many people continue to act as if races were real, obvious physical characteristics will still serve as key social markers that provide individuals and groups with packaged meanings of themselves and others. These meanings are the basis on which categorizations are made, along with expectations of what individuals and groups are like, what they are capable of, and even about their morality. Medievalists have noted that, in the context of such thinking, colour difference came to symbolize moral difference; over time, being black came to signify inferiority and immorality just as being white implied salvation. Except for the fact that stereotypes may be more subtle today, not a great deal has changed since medieval times.

Racism

Racism occurs when racial categorizations take on negative meanings, so that those meanings relegate people to subordinate positions. Along with its ideological message, racism is the practice of including individuals and groups in full participation in the social economy, or excluding them, based on imputed racial similarities or differences. Although scholars might argue that race is more accurately seen as a social construct than as a biological fact, the biological reading continues to inform the commonsense understanding, and it has real consequences for those consigned to the supposedly inferior races. And as a social construct, racism is a matter of power: the ability of some to label others, and to have those labels stick.

Ethnicity

If races or racial groups are supposed to speak to the biological aspects of human populations, ethnic groups speak to the sociocultural composition of those populations. Ethnicity has both subjective and objective features and may include one or more of the following: (a) a common history with a set of shared values and customs, language, style of dress, food, music, and other such cultural attributes; (b) a myth of common descent; (c) national or territorial claims to sovereignty; (d) an assumed inherited racial marker such as skin colour, hair texture, or facial features; and (e) some degree of economic or occupational specialization. In sum, ethnicity, a broader term than race, requires a comparative in-group/out-group dynamic.

Depending on the social environment in which they exist, ethnic groups in multi-ethnic societies face differing degrees of pressure to assimilate to the dominant culture. In those cases where they resemble the dominant group culturally, that pressure is not likely to be perceived or interpreted negatively; but, if the ethnic group in question has little in common with the dominant culture, pressure to assimilate is likely to be resisted. Because groups, ethnic or otherwise, have a tendency towards self-preservation, when such pressure appears to threaten the survival of the group the resistance is apt to be even greater. The specific form of such resistance, though, will depend on the resources available.

Resistance

Resistance can include any action, whether physical, verbal, or psychological, individual or collective, that seeks to undo the negative consequences of being categorized for racial reasons. Thus, unlike approaches that seek to portray victims of racial oppression as passive recipients of the dominant ideology and practice, the approach we take in this chapter seeks to understand how the concept "race" can be used to resist or mollify the deleterious consequences of racism. Resistance is a political act, intimately tied to the wider cultural forces that frame it. We will examine the co-optation of the label "race" by those most negatively affected by its imposition, and we will seek to understand their inversion of its meaning with a view to combatting its negative consequences.

Strategies of Resistance

There are three different strategies of resistance that are more reformist or conservative than revolutionary, because none of them sees the problem of racism as rooted in the economic practices of capitalism. As a consequence each presumes that racism can be eliminated without any fundamental alteration of the social and economic institutions of capitalist society. The first of these, which isn't usually thought of as resistance, is multiculturalism. It is in essence a *strategic retreat* because, instead of trying to be accepted and integrated into the majority group, those who take the path of multiculturalism will reject the dominant group's culture in favour of a retreat into their (supposedly) *original* culture and value system.

This strategy, known in the sociological literature as accommodation, involves the creation of imagined communities and posits a primordial attachment to them. It seeks to develop separate or culturally parallel institutions, such as small businesses, schools, churches, and community centres. The multicultural strategy usually entails the *invention* of traditions of a more pristine and noble past that is thought to have existed before their conquest and subjugation by one or another colonial power, when they were free and all were equal. Recognizing the existence of racism in the society at large, and their inability to do anything in the short run to change it, supporters of multiculturalism face an ambivalent situation. In Canada, for example, economic opportunities for immigrants are probably greater than in their native countries, and what they are in effect saying is that (a) they like their culture of origin, (b) they want, as much as possible, to retain it in their new land, and (c) they want peaceful co-existence with the dominant culture just so long as it does not intrude on their culture of origin.

That Canada is a land of great economic opportunity cannot be denied. Indeed, as previously noted in five of the last six years a United Nations survey (*Human Development Report*) ranked Canada as the best country in the world in which to live, and Canada is no doubt very attractive to prospective immigrants from all other countries, both developed and underdeveloped. Clearly there is much to be admired here, but it would be a mistake to understand Canada's enviable position internationally as resulting simply from the hard work, dedication, and decency of its citizens. For in addition to these, a key reason why Canada is able to boast one of the highest standards of living in the world is related to its status as an imperialist country with powerful allies; together they are able to dominate the resources of other countries. And it is immigrants from these latter countries, particularly the poorest, who desire most to come to Canada.

Ideologically, at the level of law and government policy, official multiculturalism, as embodied in the Canadian Multiculturalism Act, implicitly acknowledges the racism of the wider system and seeks to implement programs to rectify past wrongs. Drawing on public funds, such programs are designed to help the group involved redis-cover its "golden age," its identity, for example, as African Canadi-ans or Japanese Canadians. It matters little if claimants are ignorant of their original languages, cultures, histories, geography, and soci-ety, or that most of them have far more in common with Western values and cultures than with Japanese or African ones. When it works, however, multiculturalism is a very effective form of resis-tance to racism.

The process is greatly accelerated when multiculturalism becomes commercialized. At that point the success of this strategy is to be measured by the extent to which those outside the minority group come to embrace the symbolic culture of that group. For example, white women wearing Afro hairstyles in response to the "Black Is Beautiful" campaign, or Bo Derek's now-famous corn row hairstyle in the movie *10*, Vanilla Ice, the white rap artist that made rap music acceptable to white, middle-class youths, the Jamaicanization ("no problem, man!") of North American and Western European youth via the media of Bob Marley, reggae, Rasta, and "roots."

A second strategy of resisting racism is assimilation. The politics of assimilation dictate that the minority ethnic group accept the culture and values of the dominant group and try to "pass" into it. Assimilation is no less ideological than multiculturalism, although it may be characterized as the path of least resistance. It is resistance nonetheless. In contemporary Canadian society assimilation is best exemplified by those members of minority groups who reject mul-ticultural policies, either because these policies result from the de-mands of other organized minority groups, or because they believe that authorities are paying "official lip service" to equality among competing ethnic groups.

For ethnic groups that are visibly different from an entrenched, racist majority, assimilation is a form of naïveté, a denial of existing racism. This denial is a psychological defence mechanism, and at the personal and subjective levels, it is an attempt to soften (resist) the harshness of racism. It is most clearly evident in Neil Bissoondath's popular 1994 book, *Selling Illusions: The Cult of Multiculturalism in Canada*, in which the author opts for the comfort of obvious deception rather than accept the sting of cruel reality. The popularity of such efforts as Bissoondath's is tied to the racist establishment's eagerness to deny its racism and to point to such declarations by people "of colour" as proof that society is non-racist. Two other recent examples are Shelby Steele's *The Content of Our Character: A New Vision of Race in America*, and Dinesh D'Souza's *Illiberal Education: the Politics of Race and Sex on Campus*.

Unlike the calculated strategies of accommodation and assimilation, which involve either a strategic retreat or active self-deception, a third approach to understanding how race can be used to provide resistance to racism concerns the most commonly thought-of strategy of resistance: violent, physical engagement of the (racist) aggressor. Such violence, however, is not always clearly planned or co-ordinated, nor does it always have a clearly articulated vision of an alternative social order. Indeed, it is often spontaneous, and can spark other pockets of resistance, developing situations the authorities are unable to completely contain or control. The Palestinian "Intifada" of the early 1990s, though dismissed by some as merely "civil disobedience," is a clear instance of this form of resistance.

There are also other ways race can be used to galvanize support for resistance strategies. For example, instead of acquiescing in the dominant stereotype that holds that black is inferior and ugly, leaders of the Civil Rights Movement in the United States in the 1960s promoted the notion that "Black Is Beautiful" and exhorted their followers to "Say it loud, I'm Black and I'm proud." In the spirit of Stokely Carmichael's now-famous slogan of "Black Power," two generations of black Americans have inverted the traditional conceptions of race and colour and have militantly asserted their humanity and their political entitlement to a piece of the American pie. In Canada there are several examples of the use of violence by a targeted community to answer the force and violence of the establishment: armed stand-offs between Natives and federal authorities at Oka, Quebec, in 1991; similar stand-offs at Ipperwash, Ontario, and Gustafsen Lake, British Columbia, in 1995; the 1967 burning of computer facilities at Concordia (then Sir George Williams) University in Montreal; and Asian vigilante groups patrolling their communities in Toronto and Vancouver in the wake of racist attacks against them. In exploring the use of violence as a means of resisting racism, we will refer to Franz Fanon's 1963 classic, *The Wretched of the Earth*, which deals with the violent politics of decolonization. Multiculturalism, assimilation, and violence have two features in common: (1) all three address the question of resistance to racism, albeit in different forms, and (2) none of them advances an understanding of racism as a systemic feature of capitalist society or seeks theoretically to link racism with the dominant class and economic structures. As a consequence, all three tend to be ideologically conservative and reformist by assuming that they can defeat the forces of racism without changing too drastically the system (capitalism) that nurtures it.

Multiculturalism as Strategic Retreat

As one observer recently stated, "Canada invented multiculturalism as a national policy in 1971." Thus most Canadians will be at least superficially familiar with the term multiculturalism. The 1992 *Canadian Ethnic Studies Bulletin* reported that "77% of Canadians believe multiculturalism will enrich Canada's culture while 73% agree with the view that multiculturalism will ensure that people from various cultural backgrounds will have a sense of belonging to Canada, that it will provide greater equality of opportunity for all groups."

Nevertheless, the *Canadian Ethnic Studies Bulletin* reported that among Canadians "66% think that discrimination against non-whites is a problem," and, on the whole, "Canadians feel less comfortable with people whose origins are Indo-Pakistani, Sikh, West Indian Blacks, Arabs, Moslems than they do with persons of other origins."

It is unusual for Canadians to see multiculturalism as a strategy for resisting racism. The Canadian nation generally could be said to be in denial about the existence of racism in Canada, preferring to point fingers south of the border for examples of this scourge. Indeed, on the question of tolerance for racial and ethno-cultural diversity, nationally and internationally, Canadians tend to have a rosy understanding of themselves as enlightened, progressive, and non-racist. The political embrace of multicultural policies, both federally and provincially, is seen as evidence of such tolerance and understanding. What is not clear, though, is whether the Canadian government and people think of multiculturalism as a description of their *actual* society, the society they *wish* to have, or the society they *ought* to have.

Regardless of which of these is most accurate, the fact is that in recent years, much more so than in the past, Canada has become a racially and ethno-culturally diverse country. For a variety of reasons having to do with identity and security (e.g., occupational, residential, racial, and ethno-cultural), traditional groups in our society feel threatened and react defensively, using the various means at their disposal (e.g., economic, political, legal, sociocultural) to resist what they perceive as new "intrusions" — especially in cases of those whose physical appearance and way of life differ markedly from theirs. Facing political pressures and demands from the greater urban and industrial centres such as Toronto, Montreal, Vancouver, and Edmonton, where immigrants have tended to settle in large numbers, and recognizing the vital economic contribution that immigrants make to the entire society and economy, governments across the country in the 1960s began to draft and implement multicultural policies and programs.

Multiculturalism and multi-ethnicity have not been enthusiastically greeted by the privileged, who see them as a threat to their traditional "right" to dominate. This is not difficult to understand in a society where Anglo-European traditions and institutions dominate; where reserves have been created to contain the Aboriginal population; where, during the First World War some 8,000 Ukrainian Canadians were labelled "enemy aliens" and interned without due process in 24 camps across Canada, (Malarek 1987:11); and where in 1914 Canadian authorities prevented the landing of a freighter with 400 South Asian would-be immigrants on board (Fleras and Elliott 1992:56). This is also a country where Italian and German citizens, and over 22,000 Japanese Canadians, were placed in prison camps during the Second World War, where official immigration policy made a clear distinction between "preferred" and "non-preferred" immigrants, and where, as late as 1947, Prime Minister Mackenzie King was unequivocal, racist, and patronizing in ruling out Asians and Orientals as acceptable immigrants:

It was clearly recognised with regard to immigration from India to Canada, that the native of India is not a person suited to this country ... possessing manners and customs so unlike those of our own people, their inability to readily adapt themselves to surroundings entirely different could not do other than entail an amount of privation and suffering which render a discontinuance of such immigration more desirable in the interests of the

Indians themselves (Mackenzie King quoted in Hawkins 1991:18).

And,

The people of Canada do not wish to make a fundamental alteration in the character of their population through mass immigration. The government is therefore opposed to large scale immigration from the Orient, which would certainly give rise to social and economic problems ... (Mackenzie King quoted in Hawkins 1972:93).

During the late 1920s Canada's immigration policy designated the following as countries from which it "preferred" to receive new immigrants: Britain, Norway, Sweden, Denmark, Finland, Germany, Switzerland, Holland, Belgium, and France. Eastern Europe was designated as a "non-preferred" source; it included Austria, Hungary, Poland, Romania, Lithuania, Estonia, Latvia, Bulgaria, Yugoslavia, and Czechoslovakia. Southern European countries such as Italy and Portugal were not even mentioned.

Later, in the 1950s a similar situation faced the overwhelmingly black British West Indians who wished to come to Canada. The accepted wisdom was that they would be unable to adapt to the harsh winters, and so it would be in their best interests not to immigrate. All the evidence of West Indian "negroes" who had adapted success-fully to life in Canada prior to this time was ignored. Given this background, then, the 1993–4 involvement of the now-disbanded First Canadian Airborne Regiment in racially motivated murder and torture in Somalia is not so surprising.

Unity in Diversity

Recognizing the ethnic diversity of Canada, various levels of gov-ernment have opted for policies of multiculturalism, with a view to minimizing the prospects of ethnic conflict. Those policies were designed to address the potentially serious political fall-out for a society, economy, and labour force historically fractured along racial and ethnic lines. Public participation in such culturally diverse and colourful spectacles as Caribana, Panorama, and Caravan create a climate (if not an illusion) of political acceptance that, in the minds of minority ethnic individuals, symbolizes a way of combatting the cultural alienation, exclusion, and even rejection they face in wider

social interactions outside their communities. Such public celebrations and festivals empower them, if only momentarily, and foster a
sense of pride in their cultural traditions that they are eager to impress
upon other Canadians.

Multiculturalism is not consumed by minority groups alone. In the
calculations of politicians, the celebration of multicultural and ethnic
diversity serves as an effective mechanism of social control. Sure, it
seeks to promote a sense of tolerance and understanding among all
Canadians, but, along with the superficial pomp and celebrations of
multicultural policies and programs come other effects: they distract
citizens from the entrenched class inequalities in the wider society;
they are great for business (e.g., tourism, commercial retailers, hotels, restaurants, and the transportation industry); and they confirm
for most of us the idea that Canada is an open and accepting mosaic
of all peoples and cultures, regardless of colour, creed, or national
origin. Ethnic diversity is portrayed as highly compatible with national unity, and political speeches, which always make reference to
the rich fabric of Canadian society, can be counted on to depict that
fabric in terms of an intricate ethno-cultural tapestry.

As a means of resisting racism, then, multiculturalism has a triple
function for minority individuals and communities: (1) it enhances
their self-esteem and cultivates a favourable predisposition to the
wider society and its institutions; (2) it promotes greater understanding of difference in the minds of others, thus reducing tension
and the possibility of conflict; and (3) it holds out the promise of
equality to members of ethnic minorities, both new and old.

For most immigrants of colour and members of ethnic minority
groups, it is clear that Canada's central social, political, and economic institutions are dominated by "white" people, particularly
those of Anglo-Saxon, western European, and Jewish descent (Reitz
1990; Nakhaie 1995; Driedger 1996; Forcese 1997). Power is seen
to reside in "white" hands, and this "fact" is not lost on the members
of ethnic minority groups. Thus, even when multiculturalism pays
only lip-service to sociocultural equality, the powerless are eager to
embrace it. For them, the "white" power structure is formidable and
any (even minor) concessions to equality it grants are to be taken
very seriously. As a modern, Western, liberal society caught up in
the age of political correctness, therefore, Canada publicly and officially holds out the promise of equality to all its citizens and those
who have traditionally been least equal take the promise to heart.

A key difficulty with multiculturalism and its strategy of accom-modation, though, is that it leaves intact the very structures and institutions of domination that have traditionally been in place in this country, while seeking to encourage the building of other parallel structures and institutions that are unable to compete on an equal footing with the traditional ones. It thus gives ideological legitimacy to the latter by creating an atmosphere of equality, while simultane-ously deflecting potential political criticism of the wider system. Thus, immigrant and other minorities proudly proclaim their roots and delight in the possibility of retaining them while simultaneously professing loyalty to Canada.

Viewed in this light, multiculturalism offers the best of both worlds to ethnic minorities whose physical and cultural attributes differ significantly from the dominant norm, but who are encouraged to identify with their original cultures just so long as such identifi-cation does not interfere with core cultural values such as individu-alism and liberalism, or with the laws of the land. When made into law, multicultural policies are very effective tools for resisting ra-cism. Politically, however, proponents of such policies are essen-tially reformists who see the overall sociopolitical system, particularly as it deals with ethnic and racial minorities, as basically legitimate, though in need of some tinkering or adjusting.

Assimilation as Resistance

Another form of resisting racism is the notion of assimilation. It stands to reason that newcomers to a society will desire as smooth a process of adaptation and inclusion as possible. Where prejudice and discrimination exist, newcomers can be expected to offer different forms and degrees of resistance. They will seek to minimize their difficulties by "melting" or blending into the dominant institutions as quickly and thoroughly as possible. This implies a process of becoming "invisible" to prejudiced members of the host society, and where it works, assimilation is an effective form of resistance to racism. The questions, then, are how, where, and for whom does it work?

According to Robert E. Park's classic 1950 formulation, assimi-lation involves several progressive and irreversible stages. It comes about when new groups enter an established society and come into *contact* with groups already there. That contact is likely to lead to *competition* for scarce resources (e.g., jobs, housing, and education), and can produce *conflict*, which in turn requires various forms of *accommodation*, leading ultimately to *assimilation*. But the various stages that lead to assimilation are not inevitable. For a variety of reasons specific groups may remain at a given stage. Gordon identified seven such stages: (1) cultural or behaviourial assimilation; (2) structural assimilation; (3) marital assimilation; (4) identificational assimilation; (5) attitude receptional assimilation (absence of prejudice); (6) behaviour receptional assimilation (absence of discrimination) and (7) civic assimilation, which implies a total melting into the host or dominant culture and society (1964:71).

Thus, first there is cultural assimilation (acculturation), which sees the subordinate group gradually taking on the cultural traits (language, religion, music, food, eating habits, politics, family structure and so on) of the dominant group. As Martin Marger pointed out, however, this is not simply a one-way affair, since "there is ordinarily some exchange in the opposite direction as well" (1994:117). As can be imagined, though, the proportion of change in the opposite direction is smaller, slower, and less perceptible.

Next comes structural assimilation, the increased participation of members of the subordinate minority group in the *secondary* economic and political institutions of the dominant group. This usually involves mixing in various public and private settings, such as recreational sites, public transportation, retail shopping, political gatherings, and places of work.

In time, acculturation and structural assimilation will lead to a third stage: admission into *primary* group relations (friendship and intimacy), which can and does result in intermarriage or biological assimilation (amalgamation). In successive generations, as cultural differences evaporate and a new ethno-racial norm emerges, old patterns and practices of racism will become anachronistic.

Accompanying these three macro-structural processes of assimilation, there is a fourth, micro-interactive process known as psychological assimilation, experienced principally by first-generation immigrants and newcomers to a society. Acknowledging their powerlessness to combat the entrenched forces of prejudice and discrimination in the new society, such individuals resort to a psychological form of resistance premised on self-deception. As Marger (1994:120) has noted, with psychological assimilation, "Members of an ethnic group undergo a change in self-identity. To the extent that individuals feel themselves part of the larger society rather than an ethnic group, they are psychologically assimilated. As psychological assimilation proceeds, people tend to identify themselves decreasingly in ethnic terms."

Selling Illusions

Psychological assimilation focuses on the individual and can take different forms depending on those being assimilated and the norm they are seeking. Assimilation to a racist or xenophobic society will be far more difficult and problematic for those who are visibly different. In Canada, for example, where a "white," Anglo-Saxon appearance and Judeo-Christian beliefs and practices are dominant, immigrants who closely approximate this norm, even if they are not English speaking, will understandably have less difficulty assimilating by the second or third generation, for assimilation is both a matter of degree and a process of "melting" or disappearing into the dominant social institutions and cultural systems.

As subsequent generations acquire the language and accent of the dominant society, then, German, Italian, Polish, Ukrainian, and Greek immigrants are *free to choose* to leave their ethnic roots behind.

On the other hand, when colour and related physical features are associated with culture and national origin, for example, among East Indians, Orientals, and Africans, the challenge of assimilation is much greater. They are not as *free to choose* to use assimilation as a means for resisting racism. And so, more than 125 years after the abolition of slavery in the United States, the ideological notion of American society as a "melting pot" is not regarded seriously by either scholars or lay observers. Indeed, recent public opinion polls show that blacks and whites in the United States are more divided today than they were 30 years ago. Black people have lived in Canada and the United States for hundreds of years longer than many other immigrant groups that have long since melted into the fabric of these societies and lost their "hyphenated" identities.

Illusion, then, is a key aspect of psychological assimilation for visible minorities. Regardless of how much an individual may believe that he or she is an unidentifiable part of the larger society, that he or she is not "an ethnic," the final decision to admit lies with wider social forces and structures. Thus, even though members of ethnic minority groups may desire passionately to be accepted by the host society and may even think of themselves as assimilated in the eyes of the prejudiced majority, they might be viewed quite differently. It is this majority view that proves most consequential in the end.

A clear example of this can be seen in a Canadian context by an examination of Neil Bissoondath's *Selling Illusions: The Cult of Multiculturalism in Canada*. The author, an Indo-Trinidadian who came to Canada at the age of 18 in 1973, goes to great lengths to deny his ethnic heritage, acknowledges he is ashamed of it, despises it, and desires nothing more than to be accepted as "a Canadian." The discussion of Bissoondath here is not intended as an *ad hominem* attack. Instead, he represents "a type" and a mode of conservative thinking that is commonly encountered in the society at large, thus making it necessary to develop a critical understanding of its political origins and assumptions.

Trinidad, Bissoondath writes, is "a place where truth was formless, where one was taught to dismiss nothing and to distrust everything." Home for Bissoondath is Canada: "When I feel myself in need of comfort, security, familiarity, it is this country [Canada] — its air, its sounds, its smells, the textures of its light — that I long for. It is here, everywhere, that I find the comforts of home."

The major obstacle to his full acceptance, however, is multiculturalism, which, together with its advocacy of quota systems and equity policies in occupational, educational, and like matters, Bissoondath finds finds personally embarrassing: "I can think of few things more demeaning to me than to be offered an advantage because of my skin colour ... no matter what I have struggled to achieve ... I am still, even with the best of intentions, being viewed racially — and that is offensive to me."

Clearly, Bissoondath's problem is that he confuses equity and fairness with unfairness. Because he "made it," all others should be able to do the same; and those who do not have only themselves to blame! What he refuses to acknowledge, however, is the fact that quota systems and equity programs are not meant to reward incompetence, but rather to control the dominant society's tendency to exclude members of visible minorities regardless of their abilities.

Bissoondath's solution to the problem is to abolish multiculturalism in favour of the self-deception of being considered assimilated. Thus, "Don't call me ethnic!" was the apt headline that appeared in the October 1994 issue of *Saturday Night*, which featured prepublication excerpts of his book. Though generally ignored by intellectuals, *Selling Illusions* has been popularly received in non-academic circles by politicians, media commentators, and other lay observers who wish to deny that Canada is a racist society and are grateful whenever a "person of colour" (Bissoondath's self-description) joins the chorus of voices denouncing those who would so label Canada. For example, Marlene Nourbese Philip poignantly noted, "the dominant culture has uncritically acclaimed Bissoondath, along with his shoddy work, as their brown spokesperson" (1995:7).

To understand Bissoondath's response to multiculturalism, it is useful to see him as one who is seeking psychological assimilation. This is evidenced by his emphasis on the individual, non-structural aspects of the assimilative process. His frustration, however, comes from the fact that psychological assimilation is a two-way process, whereby (1) one identifies with the new society and (2) the latter is accepting. As a "person of colour" in a racist society, though, Bissoondath may just be fooling himself into thinking that the wider society sees beyond his ethno-racial features and their imputed meanings, and accepts him for who he is. For visibility is crucial here and those with physical markers such as skin colour are not likely to lose "ethnic status" in the minds of the majority.

Bissoondath's passionate desire to become accepted by the "white" mainstream is premised upon a denial of the racism in the society at large, and it underlines the way assimilation can be used to soften or resist the harsh consequences of racism. Thus, Bissoondath seeks to dismiss racism in Canada as a thing of the past: "Nasty things happened years ago in Canada. But that is a Canada that no longer exists. The world is no longer what it was." Exactly what the Canada of today is, however, and how it came about, he never specifies. What he does specify, though, is the fact that the new Canada must somehow resist the celebration of ethnic diversity that is multiculturalism: "To attend an ethnic festival, then, is to expose yourself not to culture but to theatre, not to history but to fantasy: enjoyable, no doubt, but of questionable significance."

In conclusion, then, Bissoondath was right to talk about "selling illusions," but he needs to acknowledge that in his economic marketplace he is both seller and buyer of illusions. In the last paragraph of his book Bissoondath revealed his unrealistic yearning for "a nation of cultural hybrids, where every individual is unique, every individual distinct. And every individual is Canadian, undiluted and undivided." If this is not illusory, then one wonders what is.

Certainly assimilation can effectively counter or resist racism in later generations for some, but for others this strategy is not a practical option. This does not mean, however, that there are not other Bissoondaths who, unable to deal with rejection, seek to distort and deny all evidence that points in its direction. It is a peaceful, conservative solution, but it remains only at the level of the individual, and of individual delusion. Politically speaking, then, if the strategy of multicultural accommodation is said to be ideologically reformist, assimilation must be said to be ideologically conservative. Indeed, Bissoondath says it best, when he notes, "Revolutionary change is illusory ... True and lasting change, then, cannot be imposed; it must come slowly, growing with experience, from within."

Resistance through Violence: The Colonial Context

Leave this Europe where they are never done talking of Man, yet murder men everywhere they find them, at the corner of every one of their own streets, in all the corners of the globe. — Franz Fanon, *The Wretched of the Earth*

Mobilization against injustice, actual or perceived, can assume many forms that are confrontational to varying degrees. These can range all the way from symbolic gestures proclaiming that "Black Is Beautiful" through peaceful protests or demonstrations, civil disobedience, public legal challenges, covert terrorism, all the way to armed engagement of the oppressor. The actual form that mobilization against injustice takes will depend on the specific situation — the resources available to the oppressed and the means at the disposal of the oppressor to retaliate. Here, we discuss that form most commonly thought of as resistance, whether to racism or any other institutional form of oppression: direct confrontation leading to the use of violence. It must be clarified at the outset, however, that not all confrontations and violence involving two or more racial groups is automatically to be blamed on racism. For it is true that when caught, lawbreakers have been known to invoke ethnic or racial identity and affiliation to claim victim status.

Nowhere is the injustice leading to violence more evident than in a colonial system on the eve of collapse. But when colonialism is in full force, the forms of resistance to its racism are more subtle. In the case of New World slavery, slaves engaged in what Gordon Lewis, a Caribbean historian at the University of Puerto Rico, has termed "covert protest," a whole range of behaviours short of escape and rebellion: "Everything from feigned ignorance, malingering, sabotage, slowed-down work habits, suicide, and poisoning of masters, on to the endless invention of attitudes that reflected a general war of psychological tensions and stresses between both sides in the master–slave relationship" (Lewis 1983:175). Realizing the futility of attacking the system head-on, most slaves devised coping mechanisms in order to survive on a daily basis.

As historian D. Hiro wrote: "They lied; they played dumb; they deliberately, yet defiantly, slowed their movements and thus reduced their work output. They perfected circumlocution as a fine art ... they developed repression of their feelings and 'playing it cool' as defense mechanisms against the system ... The slave also learned to release his frustration and misery into humour and laughter — often at himself, sometimes at his fellow slaves. For him laughter became a safety valve (1991:22)."

We know that colonialism did not come to an end with the abolition of slavery, nor did the racism and violence it inspired. As perhaps the most complete form of institutional racism, colonial domination produced a sense of rage in the colonial subject that exploded during the process of decolonization, when the colonial masters were about to exit the colony. This was poignantly captured in Franz Fanon's 1963 book, *The Wretched of the Earth* and Albert Memmi's 1965 *The Colonizer and the Colonized*, which deal with the case of Algeria and the struggles of the Algerian people to free themselves from French colonial tutelage. But as Jean-Paul Sartre noted in his Introduction to Memmi's book, rather than viewing colonialism as a "situation" it is better understood as a "system"; thus, useful generalizations can be made from the Algerian case that can cast light onto other cases in which the process of decolonization has had to come to terms with racism and violence. It is well known, as Fanon wrote, that "the well-being and the progress of Europe have been built up with the sweat and the dead bodies of Negroes, Arabs, Indians, and the yellow races," among others. Therefore, whether an African slave, an Indian indentured servant, a Chinese "coolie," or a captured native of the colony, the colonial subject was seen as "the Other," and was invested with all the negative attributes that represented the opposite of the colonizer: sexual immorality, savagery, godlessness, and evil. As Fanon wrote, "the native is declared insensitive to ethics; he represents not only the absence of values, but also the negation of values. He is, let us dare to admit, the enemy of values and in this sense he is the absolute evil."

For Fanon, decolonization is of necessity a violent process. Its point of departure is the violence committed against the colonial subject by the colonizer. In the early phase of the struggle for freedom, as the rage builds, the colonized is unable to lash out against the oppressor, and so he directs his anger at his fellows. "This is the period," Fanon writes, "when the niggers beat each other up, and the police and magistrates do not know which way to turn when faced with the astonishing waves of crime." As the struggle builds, however, the colonized native "finds out that the settler's skin is not of any more value than a native's skin; ... this discovery shakes the world in a very necessary manner." This is when the violent resistance of the colonized begins to strike fear into the heart of the colonizer, for the former come to realize that their freedom is impossible so long as colonialism and racism remain intact. Thus, Sartre minced no words when he summed up the native's options in his Preface to *The Wretched of the Earth*: "In the first days of the revolt you must kill: to shoot down a European is to kill two birds with one stone, to destroy an oppressor and the man he oppresses at the same time: there remain a dead man and a free man (1963:22)."

Violence as a Cleansing Force

To Fanon, colonialism and violence are synonymous. No process premised on invasion, plunder, and theft, that virtually exterminated the indigenous inhabitants, can legitimately expect that the victims will acquiesce forever. Resistance was as certain as the lash of the master's whip. In the process of colonial expansion, when savage nobles met noble savages, the latter were immediately made to know their place. But as the internal contradictions of colonial capitalism mounted, as the resentment of the colonized grew and the forces of decolonization began to take shape, no one could realistically expect the process to be non-violent.

For colonialism is fascism, and fascism is violence. As Memmi tells us, "There is no doubt in the minds of those who have lived through it that colonialism is one variety of fascism ... It is violence in its natural state ... and will only yield when confronted with greater violence." Thus, as the violence of colonialization confronts the counter-violence of decolonization, few are left unscarred. In the minds of the former colonized the resistance symbolized by their counter-violence is frenzied and energizing. Fanon wrote: "At the level of individuals, violence is a cleansing force. It frees the native from his inferiority complex and from his despair and inaction; it makes him fearless and restores his self-respect (1963:94)."

In today's advanced industrial countries, the violence of street gangs, of the ghettos, of the drug culture, of men against women, and the violence visited on the homeless, on the illiterate, on the poor and on the hungry, can be seen as a variation on the theme traced by

Fanon. For it is a violence turned inward: black on black, poor on poor, the desperate against the desperate. It is a blind violence. Youths on drugs, unschooled and unemployed, are casualties of a system that has created "internal colonies" in the centres of the largest cities of the West. Such phenomena as the Los Angeles riots and the Native stand-off at Oka are aspects of the violence that accompanies the process of decolonization everywhere. What is noteworthy, however, is the fact that their violence, like that described by Fanon, is often spontaneous, undirected, personal, and contained. It is not informed by a wider vision of social transformation, or the transcendence of capitalism.

Neo-colonialism and Violence: A Canadian Example

Canada has long been witness to struggles for ethno-cultural autonomy among French Canadians, particularly those of Quebec, who, even within their own country, claim to be colonized by English Canada, and who are determined to break free. This theme of "internal colonialism" and the violence it occasions was poignantly captured in Pierre Vallières' 1971 *White Niggers of America*, in which the average French Canadian was compared to the average, disenfranchised black person in the United States. In the early 1970s, Canada was plunged into a state of emergency: a violence erupted on the streets of Montreal, bombs exploded in public places, Quebec Labour Minister Pierre Laporte was murdered, and British diplomat James Cross was kidnapped and held for several days. The Front de Libération du Québec (FLQ) took responsibility for the violence and issued a manifesto outlining its philosophy, major goals, and demands.

The FLQ Manifesto

The *Front de Libération du Québec* is not the Messiah nor a modern-day Robin Hood. It is a group of Quebec workers who are committed to do everything they can for the people of Quebec to take their destiny into their own hands.

The *Front de Libération du Québec* wants the total independence of the Quebeckers brought together in a free society, purged forever of its band of voracious sharks, the big bosses who dish out patronage and their servants, who have made Quebec into their private preserve of "cheap labour" and of unscrupulous exploitation ... what is called democracy in Quebec is and always has been nothing but the victory of the election riggers ... Consequently we wash our hands of the British parliamentary system; the *Front de Libération du Québec* will never let itself be distracted by the electoral crumbs that the Anglo-Saxon capitalists toss into the Quebec barnyard every four years. Many Quebeckers have realized the truth and are ready to take action ... We have had our fill of taxes which Ottawa's man in Quebec wants to hand out to the English-speaking bosses to give them "incentive" to speak French, to negotiate in French. Repeat after me: "Cheap labour is *main d'oeuvre a bon marché.*"

Working people in the factories, in mines and in the forests; working people in the service industries, teachers, students and unemployed: Take what belongs to you, your labour, your determination and your freedom. And you, the workers at General Electric, you make the factories run; you alone are capable of producing, without you, General Electric is nothing!

Working people of Quebec, begin today to take back what belongs to you; take yourselves what is yours. You alone know your factories, your machines, your hotels, your universities, your unions, do not wait for a miracle organization.

Make your revolution yourselves in your neighbourhoods, in your workplaces ... You alone are capable of building a free society.

We are Quebec workers and we will go to the end ... we want, with all the people, to replace this slave society with a free society, functioning of itself and for itself, a society open to the world.

Our struggle can only be victorious. Not for long can one hold in misery and scorn, a people once awakened.

Long live Free Quebec!

Long live our comrades the political prisoners! Long live the Quebec Revolution!

Long live the *Front de Libération du Québec!*

What is interesting about the FLQ Manifesto is that while it called for an end to Anglo-Saxon capitalism, it did not call for the abolition of capitalism per se; nor did it mention anything about socialism. It is as though the authors were thinking in ethno-linguistic terms, supposing that somehow French-speaking capitalists would be kinder to French-speaking workers than English-speaking capitalists were. The underlying reformism is unmistakable here, and it goes to the heart of our earlier observation that resistance is not always critically informed or possessed of a clear alternative vision of the society.

Conclusion

Our central theoretical point of departure for this chapter concerns debate over the role of race versus class, and which is more salient in terms of political consciousness and opposition in capitalist society. On one hand are those, like Robert Miles, who refuse even to give legitimacy to the concept "race" by treating it as a real or meaningful category. He criticized those who "have, perversely, prolonged the life of an idea that should be explicitly and consistently confined to the dustbin of analytically useless terms" (Miles 1989:72). Miles, therefore, favours a stricter class approach to analyzing social inequality under capitalism, and agrees with Canadian sociologist Peter Li who argues that "the fundamental source of inequality under capitalism is, in the Marxian view, social class." Li also maintains that other forms of inequality are basically derived from class, and in this context he notes that "This is the way race and ethnicity should be understood under the capitalist system" (Li 1988:48). On the other hand, there are those, like the controversial and outspoken sociologist at the University of London, Paul Gilroy, who feel that race must be retained as an analytic category not because it corresponds to any biological or epistemological absolutes, but because it draws attention to the power that collective identities acquire by means of their roots in tradition. In other words, even if primordial membership in a race is a purely imaginary phenomenon, even if race consciousness is false consciousness, and even if races are social constructs and not biological realities, so long as people in power continue to treat them as real, they will have real consequences for all involved. One cannot presume that the public is sociologically informed on all such matters.

It seems, then, that the most fruitful approach to the intellectual stand-off is to recall the words of Trinidadian historian C.L.R. James, who is committed to the class position, but who cautions us that in dealing with capitalism and imperialism: "The race question is subsidiary to the class question in politics, and to think of imperialism in terms of race is disastrous. But to neglect the racial factor as merely incidental is an error only less grave than to make it fundamental" (quoted in Gilroy 1987:15).

Class is fundamental to the Marxist understanding of resistance against social inequality under capitalism; but unlike orthodox Marxists, who hold that race consciousness is merely secondary, a matter of "false consciousness," neo-Marxists correctly leave the door open to the possibility that the class struggle can be advanced by embracing the race struggle (or even the gender struggle) at strategic moments. For as Gilroy reminded us, "Racism does not, of course, move tidily and unchanged through time and history. It assumes new forms and articulates new antagonisms in different situations." This is a call for empirical research to inform theoretical insight, because different forms of oppression demand different strategies of resistance. But under capitalism, especially when oppression is perceived as being based on race and racism, contextualizing race within the class struggle offers a broader, and hence possibly more viable, base for resistance. There are, however, no automatic guarantees of successful resistance, for we are dealing here with a question of *process*. Thus, resistance, whether spontaneous or planned, is a two-way street: each oppositional act of resistance can expect to provoke counter-resistance.

Clearly, then, the strategy is not to surrender to the forces of racism in Canada or elsewhere, but to prepare better for the challenges of resistance. This implies more study of, and research into, the various available strategies that can be used to meet the conditions at hand, and the efficacy of each. We must not be deluded into thinking that a mere tinkering with surface manifestations of racism and racial inequalities will rid society of such a deep-rooted social problem.

4

Gender Inequalities in Canada

Few issues currently generate as much interest, debate, or acrimony as does inequality between women and men. Given the attention this topic has received, one would think that we would have moved further towards consensus about how society might be structured in a more equitable fashion. Yet, the persistence of gender inequities makes the problem appear in certain ways intractable, and at times Canadians as a whole seem confused when "gender" is at issue. It is within this context of antagonism and frustration that we will briefly analyze gender relations in Canada with a view to helping men and women recognize some of their common interests and develop the political will to resolve this important issue. But, in order to act upon their common interests, men and women must understand who actually benefits from the gender inequalities and tensions that characterize contemporary social relations.

Many Canadians born in the latter half of the twentieth century were, or are, optimistic about the potential for women to share equally in the wealth and power of Canadian society. However, for many this optimism waned in the 1980s, as it became apparent that the ideals of the 1960s were not being fully realized. In fact, the contrast between the ideals of the 1960s and the realities of the 1990s suggests that there is a *stall* in progress towards equality in Canada, and in other countries attempting the same changes. This is evident not only in persisting forms of workplace segregation and wage disparity, but in a lack of consensus over what should be done to correct them. Moreover, there is now even a lack of consensus among academic feminists regarding what form "gender equality" should take in society.

In our view, the stall itself — as well as the lack of consensus about what to do about it — are in part attributable to the fact that certain workplace inequalities are necessary conditions for the survival of advanced industrial capitalism. Historically, women have constituted one of several groups of cheap labour targeted by capitalists. In a sense, gender inequality is good for contemporary capitalism because it allows profit margins to be sustained. Indeed, the very notion that men and women are "opposite" sexes is "good" for capitalism.

Explaining Gender Inequality: A Materialist Approach

Much has been written on gender inequality in Canada and elsewhere, documenting inequities in the workplace, in education, and in the wider society. This literature adopts a number of perspectives, including biological and "idealist" explanations of persisting inequalities. Our approach to understanding the persistence of gender inequalities follows the position laid out in the previous three chapters. That is, we adopt a materialist position towards gender inequalities that looks to the class structure of the society — the distribution of wealth and privilege — to see what objective conditions obtain for different people as they earn their daily livelihoods. We see biological and idealist approaches to the issue as limited in their ability to explain how the structure of inequality originated and why it is resistant to change.

Because our approach is focused on material conditions, we will not address all of the contributions to the literature on gender inequalities in Canada. In particular, we do not incorporate approaches that fail to treat inequality as an inevitable condition of capitalist society, from which certain groups predictably benefit. A materialist analysis of gender inequalities takes as its point of departure the physical organization of work performed by women both in the home and in the labour force. This is in turn related to the way employers' interests are articulated with the economic needs of the family. What work is actually performed by women and who, ultimately, gains from it? Ideas and ideologies about gender roles and relations emerge out of the objective and practical conditions (both physical and social) under which people struggle to produce and reproduce their existence. The important point, therefore, is that material conditions and struggles *give rise* to beliefs and ideologies (and not vice versa), as human beings fight to define themselves and their worlds.

One objective condition of industrial capitalism is the constant demand for reserve armies of unpaid or cheap labour, which make possible continued high rates of exploitation. The larger these armies, the more wages can be suppressed, and the more profit can be extracted. Competition dictates that a capitalist enterprise which fails to secure the average rate of profit will not survive very long. Therefore, owners of enterprises most at risk are also most likely to try to maintain conditions that maximize their profit, especially conditions that ensure that certain workers are employed as cheaply as possible. For historical reasons, women have constituted both unpaid and cheap labour throughout the era of industrial capitalism. They have provided unpaid labour in the home to reproduce and maintain labour power, at virtually no expense to capitalists. During the early industrial period, women were pressured to spend their married lives bearing and raising children, all the while emotionally supporting their husbands — producing, reproducing, and maintaining the labour force. Single women also provided cheap labour in low-paying factory jobs, often enduring horrid working conditions and abuses. Following the periodic ups and downs of the capitalist economy in the more recent industrial period, even married women have been called upon to enter and exit the workforce under similar conditions.

Bearing all this in mind, let us now look at the history of gender inequality in Canada and see how it can inform our understanding of the current situation. But in order to prepare readers for the materialist analysis that follows, we begin with a discussion of two key concepts: (1) the gendered division of labour and (2) the separation between the public and private spheres of labour.

The Fundamental Division of Labour

All societies organize themselves in ways that assign different tasks to various members, often on the basis of visible attributes like sex and age. This assignment of tasks contributes to survival or even affluence. Sometimes the assignment is hierarchical, reflecting an unequal sharing of the fruits of collective labour. In some societies, tasks are performed side by side in the same area or sphere; in other societies, tasks are performed in separate spheres.

A division of labour by gender appears to be fundamental to all societies. Because physical-sexual attributes are the most immediately apparent attributes, it is assumed that they are the most obvious bases for assigning people different roles. Accordingly, the biological capacity for childbearing has been seen as a feature that might push groups to assign women to one set of tasks and men to another. And, because only women bear children, some theorists believe that men were viewed in some societies as more expendable. Accordingly, men were more likely to be warriors and hunters, the high risk-takers for the community. Another common explanation holds that pregnancy, breastfeeding, and care for the very young tied women more closely than men to the home. Variations and exceptions to these generalizations are found in different cultures and at different times, but factors such as these may have contributed to the division of labour with which modern Canadians are attempting to deal.

Some societies are doing a better job dealing with this legacy than others, but so far none has managed to eradicate the gendered division of labour. One way to understand why this is so and how it might be changed is to examine societies where women have traditionally enjoyed higher status, as well as those where the status of women has improved.

Sociohistorical analysis suggests that an important condition needs to be present for any "group" to enjoy high status in any society, whether it be a small tribal group or a large society: their roles in the division of labour need to be recognized as making a *direct* contribution to the material welfare of their community. Regardless of how fair this may seem from the lens of the 1990s, if women as a group are not recognized as contributing directly to the material wealth of the community, history suggests that their status will not be high. This principle applies not just to women, but also to other groups, like the young. This sociohistorical principle can serve as a benchmark in tracing how the status of women has changed over the centuries in Canada.

The Private and Public Spheres

In the preindustrial era, most labour was performed in the household. For the average (non-capitalist) colonist, most of the necessities of life were grown, made, or extracted in or around the homestead. In the overall economy, the household was primarily a unit of production, while "consumption" was limited to the essentials of day-to-day sustenance and shelter. In this setting, women, men and children worked side by side. However, during the late nineteenth and early twentieth centuries, industrial capitalism radically transformed the household economy. According to Rifkin (1995), "consumption" is a part of the consumer society as a result of efforts by manufacturers to encourage people to buy their products. One meaning of this word is "to waste."

Driven by the requirements of the new industrial order, two spheres of labour emerged: the "private sphere" and the "public sphere." Patricia Lengerman and Ruth Wallace, two American sociologists, define these spheres as follows: "*Public sphere* refers to the complex, bureaucratically organized institutions of modern life: the economy, the state, formal education, organized religion, the professions and unions, the mass media of communication and entertainment ... *Private sphere* refers to the less formal, emotionally more open networks of social relationships that coexist with the public sphere: marriage, family, kin, neighbourhood, community, friendship" (1985:107).

Lengerman and Wallace also observed that societal power lies in the public sphere, while the private sphere exercises less formal power and is heavily affected by the public one. Moreover, they argued that the "hallmark of the conventional gender arrangements is that women have restricted access to the public sphere, while men have restricted participation in the private sphere." Much of the women's movement in Western societies has sought to give women equal access to the public sphere and to encourage men to take a more active role in the private one. It has been very difficult to coax many men into the private sphere. In Sweden, for example, where the "Swedish experiment" has been attempting for some 30 years to accomplish this as one of its goals, little success has been achieved. Only a small percentage of Swedish men have embraced the private sphere to the extent that the majority of women do the public sphere. For details, see Jacobsson and Alfredsson (1993), and The Swedish Institute (1992).

Given a history of segregation of men and women into separate spheres, it is understandable that people in industrial-capitalist societies have tended to base their identities on the roles available to them. To understand the persistence of gender inequalities, therefore, we need first to understand how identities are shaped around certain roles. We believe that male and female identities have been manipulated in ways that serve the interests of capital, and that sustain gender inequality. However, in the twentieth century, especially in its past two decades, roles have changed dramatically. Women have become increasingly active in the public sphere, while at the same time there has been a widespread reassessment and reworking of gender arrangements in the private sphere. Over this period, life chances and experiences have changed for both men and women, reflecting a reconvergence of the spheres separated by industrial capitalism. This applies especially to those making the effort to move from one sphere to the other. Notably, though, in every Western country so far studied, more women are doing so than men. Nevertheless, belief in the "rightness" of traditional segregated arrangements appears to persist: what "is" or "has been" is translated into what "ought to be" — (see Lengerman and Wallace 1985:45–6, 57, n5). This type of thinking among the lay public puts pressure on men and women to stay in separate spheres as if it is their rightful place (reinforcing the "ideology of gender"; Côté and Allahar 1994), but as Lengerman and Wallace show, it *does not follow* logically that to speak of these spheres sociologically is to attempt to relegate men and women to their traditional ones.

The Gendered Division of Labour: The Material Basis

From the perspective of the 1990s, it is easy to look at the past as one of a pervasive patriarchal oppression of women. While it is true that Canadian society has a history of patriarchy, it is instructive to separate the material basis of the division of labour from its ideological basis.

As noted in Chapter 3, before Europeans began exploring and settling what is now Canada, Natives had occupied these lands for thousands of years. By most accounts, the gendered division of labour was reasonably equitable, with few stable distinctions between private and public spheres or labour. Because Native women played a key part in contributing to the material well-being of their communities, they enjoyed a status comparable to Native men. In many Native tribes, women also participated in political affairs.

By modern standards, the earliest European settlers in Canada faced severe conditions: poor housing, poor diet, infectious diseases, and poor hygiene, not to mention long, cold winters during which food grown in short summers was carefully rationed. Natives often helped settlers adjust to these stark conditions, ensuring their survival. Most of the earliest pioneers were "dirt farmers" who made what they could out of often rocky and barren land. Many saw friends and family die on the voyage across the Atlantic or suffer untimely deaths from injuries or infections. Contending with meagre material conditions, early European settlers were typically concerned with the means of survival. It is easy to underplay the relevance of this in the 1990s, when much of the population now take their means of survival for granted. Instead of being concerned with these "lower order" needs, much of the population is now more concerned with "higher order" needs associated with a sense of community, and their own self-esteem and self-actualization. For according to Abraham Maslow (1954), humans experience a hierarchy of needs, from lower order survival needs to higher order self-esteem and self-actualization needs. When a lower order need is not being fulfilled, people focus on it and are not concerned with higher order ones. However, when lower order needs are met, people expect more, including experiencing self-esteem and self-actualization from their jobs. If Maslow is correct about this, we can understand better the "other directedness" of many people, who focus on others because they derive their sense of self-esteem from others. Some work-related stresses associated with "office politics" seem to be associated with the playing out of people's attempts to meet their higher order needs in competition with others.

A recent Statistics Canada analysis provides considerable insight into the life chances and life experiences of the average Caucasian woman and man over the past three centuries. According to their analysis, a pioneer born in 1700 had a life expectancy of between 30 and 35 years. Over the next four generations this improved, but only to the point where by 1831 men had a life expectancy of 40 years and women of 42. It took another four generations before life expectancies resembled those which we now take for granted. Among those born in the 1990s, females can expect to live about 81 years and males some 75 years.

The 1993 Statistics Canada study also noted that very high infant mortality rates had severe implications for the childbearing role of women. Even in the 1800s only about two-thirds of women survived to childbearing age. Those who survived to age 50 bore, on average, 10 children by the time they were 40. By the time they completed their childbearing, most of their expected life had been played out. Many women did not see their children grow into adulthood. This picture is dramatically different from the one faced by contemporary women. Women born in the early 1950s have only one or two children, and have devoted only about two years of their lives to pregnancy and early infant care. If we subtract these two years from their longer life expectancies and ignore mandatory retirement, contemporary women actually have more of their lives available than men for participation in the public sphere of society, particularly paid work.

In the earliest pioneer days, there was very little paid labour, of course, because most men *and* women worked the land for food and made their own goods. Production took place in the home and the family was the basic unit of production. In fact, "home" and "work" were difficult to distinguish. Even those who worked for a wage often did so in a family establishment, living with the family employing them.

The family remained the basic unit of production in Canada for more than two centuries. During this time markets grew, but many men and women still made some products in the home to sell in the market (they sold what was surplus to their own needs). Historians note that in this setting, men and women were more or less equal partners. This domestic production meant that women were valuable economic partners in the struggle for survival, and this was generally acknowledged.

Paid labour grew slowly, and it was largely males who performed it. The paid labour force of the eighteenth and nineteenth centuries comprised mainly *young* males, who worked on average only about two decades, before they died. But more germane to the impending decline in the status of women was a rapid disappearance of the household economy of production along with a rapid rise in industrial capitalist production.

By the early 1900s domestic production had disappeared in much of Canada. Few households could produce what they needed for survival, and work increasingly took place outside the home. Factories, offices, and stores replaced home-based production, increasingly segregating workers. Consequently, industrial capitalism created a division of the earlier labour process into two discrete spheres: the private, domestic sphere in which labour power itself (children) was produced and maintained by women; and the public, industrial sphere, where goods and services were produced mainly by men for the commodity markets.

In the first part of the twentieth century these processes accelerated, helped by increased mechanization and automation, and by compulsory education. With the mechanization of agriculture, which displaced workers, more men were drawn into factories and offices; women were assigned to operate new domestic technologies in the home; and as children were required to attend school to later and later ages, the menial labour they had once performed in the home was taken up by adult women. In short, the new role of "housewife" put the burden of maintaining the domestic unit (now a unit of consumption rather than production) almost entirely on women. Accordingly, their status fell dramatically, as they were left out of the production process, which was recognized as contributing *directly* to the collective wealth.

A century ago, about 15% of the paid labour force in Canada was made up of women, who were largely young and unmarried. Those who worked in the public sphere received low wages and had limited opportunity for advancement, so life in the private sphere was more appealing. In fact, what has been called the "cult of true womanhood" and the "cult of domesticity" bombarded women with the message that their "true" place was in the home having and raising children, tending to their husbands' needs, and not competing with men for jobs. And married women were not to engage in paid labour. The ideal woman was pure, pious, and submissive. Because of these influences, at the turn of the last century only about 3% of married women in Canada worked for wages outside the home. The concept of the ideal woman was buttressed by the media of the time (mainly magazines and pamphlets), and by the educational system, which channelled women into the study of home economics, even through advanced study. It would be several decades before women would make any meaningful gains in the public sphere.

Compared with their forebears, contemporary men face quite different circumstances. The average male can expect to spend over 40 years in the paid-labour force, and very few will be engaged in agricultural labour or any work that provides for self-sufficiency. In other words, the contemporary male sells his labour power to survive and has little choice about it. The history of the labour movement tells us that many men resented the exploitation that went along with the appropriation of their labour power. Many were forced off the homestead that was their heritage, and trades workers and craft workers found their economic functions lost or diminished by mass production. With their skills made obsolete, many men were forced to take on undignified manual labour or factory work at exploitive wages, often working under dangerous conditions. Men felt pressure to provide all the money necessary to support their families, so they needed to find employment that would provide a sufficient "living wage." To add insult to injury, many could not do this adequately, and as a result they were often made to feel ashamed.

Gender comparisons of life expectancy suggest that, in spite of material gains, industrialization has been costly for men's physical well-being. For those born in 1831 there was a two-year difference in the life expectancies of Canadian women and men. However, by 1951 this difference had increased to eight years. Despite any advantages in status that paid labour may have given men over women during this period, therefore, industrialization appears to have been "harder" on them than on women.

Given this historical–demographic context, we can now understand somewhat better the painful transition to industrial capitalism that women — and men — have experienced. Most men working in the paid labour force of the late twentieth century have little knowledge or awareness of earlier times, when labour was less alienating, that is, when they had control over how they spent their time and what they produced. This alienation of the industrial capitalist workplace is simply taken by most as a normal state of affairs. Being a successful wage-earner came to be a defining feature of the identity of twentieth-century men. At the same time, women were conditioned to be "good homemakers" and to believe that involvement in paid labour would mean they were neglecting their family duties and taking work away from men who had families to support. These conditions have combined to help create a sense of competitiveness among many men today in terms of sharing paid labour with women who have been attempting to take their rightful place in the public sphere.

The Gendered Division of Labour: Ideological Justification

Material conditions give rise to beliefs that people use to create meaning in their lives. Generally, when inequality is involved in the origin and maintenance of these material conditions, these beliefs justify those conditions and disguise their true nature. And, such beliefs often congeal to form a full-blown ideology, a body of thought difficult to contest, because ideologies tend to be emotionally linked to the identities of those affected by material conditions.

In the past, religion provided part of the ideological justification for the gendered division of labour. In Western societies, this has included a hierarchy rooted in the form of patriarchy in which the father was the head of the family. (Thus there was also a hierarchy among males, with the father having power over his sons.) Today, religion still provides an acceptable justification for many people, but this is on the decline, given the increasingly secular ethos of the society. Now, rather than having an explicit religious justification, for many people ideologies have scientific and political justifications. In these forms, the ideologies are often more implicit, that is, they have become an integral part of the culture which many people simply take for granted as "normal." Thus, the contemporary form of patriarchy influencing many Canadians does not rely on a "supreme father" image, but on a more subtle belief system that legitimates male dominance in areas like job segregation and differential wages.

Contemporary patriarchy has been challenged by recent laws forbidding various forms of discrimination. Yet, it persists, in part because it is difficult for individual women and men to change the way they have been taught to think. Indeed, implicit ideologies can put tremendous pressure on individuals because of their intangibility. It can be difficult for individuals to articulate just why they think and behave in a given manner. To make matters worse, digging deeper into motivations can be a threatening and anxiety-producing exercise. But we can easily see contemporary patriarchy in the behaviours of some employers, whether male or female (who believe that men deserve a living wage but women do not, that there is "women's work" and "men's work," or that men make better managers), as well as in the "gendering" of commodities marketed by modern advertising and commercial firms.

The challenge for the twenty-first century, then, will be to deal with a cultural legacy in which people have seen it as "normal" for women to be relegated to the private sphere of the family and men to the public sphere of work and politics. This legacy of role segregation has been, and continues to be, internalized by many men — and by many women. We have referred to this as the "ideology of gender." It permeates contemporary culture, from educational curricula to the messages of the mass media.

Even in the "enlightened" time of the late twentieth century, we find that many young Canadian men and women have been brought up to believe cultural myths based on the "proper" roles of men and women. As they internalize these myths into their own value systems they reproduce remnants of patriarchy and (may) eventually pass them on to their children. During their teens many young people undergo a phase of "gender intensification" as they form central aspects of their adult identities. Few people of any age seem to take the time to reflect on the fact that gendered roles may have emerged out of the material conditions of survival, or as a response to the needs of industrial capitalism. Today, however, there is no justification for gender segregation into private and public spheres, either in the survival of the species or in any historical necessity associated with industrial capitalism.

Perhaps the ability of the ideology of gender to resist change can be explained, in part, by the fact that it is so entrenched in modern industrial society. In fact, it took great effort to manufacture this ideology, beginning back in the 1800s with the concept of the ideal woman and intensified during the 1920s as advertisers perfected their techniques of influence.

The ideology of gender is the result of a concerted effort on the part of particular interests, mainly capitalist, to "manufacture consent" and manipulate public consciousness on certain issues. It has been very profitable for business interests to ensure that males and females remain in somewhat segregated spheres. For example, males and females to various extents view each other as "opposites" who need attracting, so a whole set of products are sold to people under the pretext that they will attract the "opposite sex." Many men and women may not be consciously attempting to attract the other sex, but are simply trying to "display" their gender in ways they have been taught by advertisers and the media. These products amount to billions of dollars in sales every year.

Thus, we have a society in which expensive display and courting rituals are repeated daily and are nurtured and maintained through the messages of advertising, movies, magazines, novels, and television programs. Simply stated, during this century people have been made to believe that this is the "normal" way for men and women to deal with their attraction to each other. This is part and parcel of the ideology of gender, with which capitalists manipulate vestiges of patriarchy for their own purposes. But in doing so, they maintain a barrier between women and men, thereby sustaining the ideological confusion between sexual differences and gender inequalities.

Gender in the Late Twentieth Century

During the early history of industrial capitalism, the life courses of men and women "diverged." More recently, their life courses have "converged." With the advent of widespread wage labour and the mass production of commodity goods, the domestic unit changed from being one of production to one of consumption, with women left in the home as unpaid labour to tend to children and their husbands. The average woman and man increasingly occupied separate spheres. This material condition was justified by, among other things, an ideology that has been called the "cult of true womanhood," in which married women were expected to provide a "haven" for their husbands and children from the cruel world of industrial capitalism.

Changes over the past several decades suggest, however, that a life-course convergence is occurring for younger Canadian men and women. This can be seen in a movement towards greater sharing and overlap of the private and public spheres. In fact, with each successive post–Second World War age group, the life courses of young women and men are becoming more and more alike. This convergence is quite apparent in education, in work and career opportunities, and in family life. It means there are increased possibilities for identity formation. That is, both women and men have time to explore and develop interests, and greater freedom to base commitments on personal choices and personal fulfilment: they have more freedom to choose sexual partners and explore their sexuality, as well as to develop lifestyles suited to their talents and inner needs. But, it is clear that the legacy of the past separation of the public and private spheres persists for many women and men. It is to the current state of the sharing and segregation of the spheres that we now turn.

The Public Sphere

In the 1994 third edition of their book *The Double Ghetto: Canadian Women and Their Segregated Work*, Pat Armstrong and Hugh Armstrong made a compelling case that women have not progressed in the public sphere of paid labour as far as many believe, particularly since midcentury (their point of reference is 1941). They argued that although women's participation in the labour force has tripled since then, so that now the participation rate of younger women approximates that of men, their participation does not reflect an equal share of community material resources. In their view, the segregation of women's and men's work continues, and despite the momentous changes in the sexual composition of the labour force, women are still greatly overrepresented in the least attractive jobs in "industries and occupations characterized by low pay, low recognized skill requirements, low productivity, and low prospects for advancement."

Earlier in this century, women's participation in the labour force was largely dictated by "market demand." When they were needed, for example, during the Second World War, they were readily recruited by employers. But this recruitment was in a buyers' market in which many women functioned as a reserve of cheap labour, to be called upon only as capitalist production demanded. As Armstrong and Armstrong noted, a "large supply of women at home without paid work helps ensure that extra workers will be available when needed." In this buyers' market, women filled gaps in the labour supply and were offered low wages and benefits, often on a part-time or part-year basis. With their ideological anchoring in the private sphere of family responsibility and their belief that it was inappropriate to compete with "breadwinning" men, most women apparently did not feel that they were in a position to bargain over wages and working conditions.

Employers capitalized on this ideological anchoring by paying only enough to constitute a "second income" for the family. And women did not have an organized support system, as did men with their unions, which attempted to help men maintain a living wage to support their families. Even as recently as 1994 women made up about 70% of part-time workers (about 25% of women with jobs, compared with 10% of men with jobs), while more than 30% of these workers preferred full-time work but could only obtain it part-time, an increase of 12% from 1989. Even women employed full-time all year work fewer hours than do men in the same situation.

Armstrong and Armstrong also held that the willingness of women as a whole to provide this supplementary form of labour has decreased sharply, as has their willingness to be the primary agents in the private sphere. They argued that only a minority of women now leave the labour force after the birth of their first child, and when they do they stay out for only a short period. And, because of today's low birthrate — women commonly have only one or two children — most women now hold paid jobs for most of their adult lives. They concluded that women's "labour force participation patterns have become more and more like those of men." Table 4.1 shows the effect of raising children on labour force participation.

In spite of these changes, women's increased participation in the public sphere still seems to be dictated by the needs of the advanced capitalist workplace for a reserve army of cheap labour. Many employers have taken advantage of the legacy of patriarchy, which includes notions of "women's work" and ideological ties to the private sphere. Hence, we find that many of the jobs performed by women are extensions of work performed in the home: seeing to the basics of daily functioning (clerical work), ensuring that the basic needs of others are met (service work), cleaning, preparing and serving food, making and mending clothing, teaching and caring for the young, disabled, and elderly. In addition, employers have capi-

Table 4.1

Labour Force Participation Rates of Women by Age and Presence of Children in 1981 and 1991 (percentages)

	Age group							
	15–24		25–34		35–44		45–54	
	1981	1991	1981	1991	1981	1991	1981	1991
All women	61	65	66	79	64	80	56	72
With no children at home	64	66	89	91	79	85	61	71
With children	44	52	54	70	61	78	53	72
At least one child under age 6	44	52	49	67	47	69	37	61
Aged 6 and over only	63	72	66	77	64	80	55	73

Source: Logan and Belliveau (1995).

talized on the poorer bargaining position of older women, who have had less education and less paid-work experience.

We can also trace the rise in women's paid employment to the rise of the service sector. In the early 1950s about 67% of those employed in service industries were women, but by the 1990s this had increased to 80%. These service jobs tend to be low skill and labour intensive, and as such, low paid. But, to make matters worse, employers have replaced labour with machines whenever profitable, so many women have found themselves taking low-paying jobs in a growth area only to be displaced by a machine (often, in recent times, by a computer). Their status as a reserve army of labour continues, despite the fact that most women no longer have the same ideological anchoring to the private sphere, and they now have more education and job experience.

Table 4.2 helps us understand the situation women (and men) face in the workplace of the 1990s. It provides a breakdown of occupations by sex for the years 1982 and 1994, allowing us to examine

Table 4.2

Distribution of Occupations for 1982 and 1994:
Percentages of Women and Men Employed in Each
Occupation and Women as a Percentage of Employees in
Each Occupation

	1982			1994		
	Women	Men	Women /Men	Women	Men	Women /Men
Managerial/ Administrative	6.0	10.2	29.3	12.7	13.8	43.1
Natural sciences/ engineering	1.3	5.3	14.9	1.7	5.9	19.2
Social sciences/ religion	2.0	1.8	42.7	3.3	2.1	56.8
Teaching	6.1	3.0	58.9	6.9	3.3	63.4
Doctors/ dentists	0.3	0.8	18.3	0.5	0.9	32.1
Nursing/ therapy/ health related	8.8	1.1	84.7	9.1	1.2	86.1
Artistic/ literary/ recreational	1.4	1.6	38.6	2.2	2.1	46.4
Clerical	34.2	6.4	78.8	26.8	5.4	80.2
Sales	10.1	10.8	39.7	10.1	9.9	45.7
Service	18.1	10.7	54.2	17.1	11.0	56.2
Primary	2.8	8.0	19.6	2.1	6.4	21.3
Manufacturing	6.4	19.8	18.4	4.8	17.3	18.5
Construction	0.2	9.3	1.4	0.3	9.3	2.4
Transportation	1.5	6.0	5.9	0.8	6.2	9.2
Material handling/crafts	1.8	5.2	19.3	1.6	5.0	21.0
Total	100.0	100.0	41.2	100.0	100.0	45.2

Source: Statistics Canada, *Women in Canada*, 3rd ed. (1995).

recent trends. Most striking here is the concentration of women into five occupations that mirror work done by women in the private sphere (clerical, sales, service, teaching, and nursing related): 77.1% of employed women were in these five occupational groups in 1982 and 70.0% in 1994, compared with 33.0% and 30.8% of men, respectively. Thus, in terms of life chances and life choices, contemporary women still face greater restrictions than do men, pointing to a limitation of the life-course convergence that we have been discussing. In other words, the "homogenization" of women noted a quarter century ago is still a factor in the lives of many women of the 1990s. But, there is some room for optimism when we look at changes between 1982 and 1994 in terms of growth in non-traditional occupations such as management/administration, natural science/engineering, and medicine/dentistry. However, it is unclear how much of this "growth" actually represents job redefinition (e.g., when a clerical worker is assigned "management" duties at the same pay).

Hughes (1995) traces the growth of women in the experienced labour force with census data, noting that between 1986 and 1991 men's participation in the labour force remained stable at about 77%, while women's increased from 55.4% to 60.7% (increases took place for all age groups). By 1991 women in the labour force had almost as many higher educational credentials as men. However, their increasing participation in the labour force and their increasing accreditation in male-dominated fields did not necessarily translate into employment in non-traditional occupations. In 1971, 86% of women were in traditionally female occupations, but by 1991 this had only dropped to 78%, with women concentrated in about one-quarter of all occupations (132 out of 484). The few occupations that experienced a significant growth in female participation between 1986 and 1991 were optometry, services and financial management, osteopathy and chiropractics. Women who moved into male-dominated occupations worked more hours than other female workers, but fewer hours than their male counterparts. They also tended to be younger, were less likely to have a university degree, and were paid less than men.

When we focus on wages, a complex picture emerges. Table 4.3 shows that the "gender gap" in wages has been a more or less constant factor over this century. Although "real wages" have quadrupled (Rashid 1994) for both men and women, women have consistently made between only 50% and 60% of what men have. Between 1940 and 1970 wages increased between 30% and 40% per decade,

Table 4.3

Real Average Annual Wages for Canadian Women and Men, 1920–1990, and Percentage Difference

	Women	Men	Women/Men (%)
1920	4,100	7,500	55
1930	5,000	8,300	60
1940	4,700	9,600	49
1950	7,400	12,800	58
1960	10,000	18,500	54
1970	13,700	26,200	52
1980	15,700	29,900	53
1990	17,900	29,800	60

Source: Rashid (1994) Based on adjusted 1990 dollars for all workers (full-time, part-time, full-year, and part-year).

an increase that slowed in the 1970s and stalled in the 1980s. During the 1980s men's "real average annual wage" decreased slightly, while women's rose 14%, (more or less duplicating the rise in women's wages in the 1970s). This increase in women's earning power is most likely a result of their improved education and work experience.

Table 4.4 provides a breakdown of women's earnings by age and education for 1993. It is apparent that both factors influence women's earning potential: younger women and those with more education tend to have the greatest earning power. Among the youngest women in the workforce, university-educated women earn a full 84% of what men in the same category make. From these figures it appears that progress has recently been made towards wage parity. But some would argue that previous estimates were based on the erroneous assumption that annual wage estimates took full account of the number of hours worked. Recent surveys indicate that employed men work full-time, on average, three to four hours more each week than do women employed full-time. An examination of the annual salaries of university graduates from the class of 1990 shows that female graduates are paid slightly better than their male counterparts with

Table 4.4

Percentage of Earnings of Women Working Full-Time Compared with Men, by Education and Age, in 1993

	Age group		
Level of education	25–34	35–44	45–54
All women	76	72	67
Some secondary	63	62	60
Graduated high school	74	68	67
Some post-secondary	65	67	51
Post-secondary diploma	75	76	73
University degree	84	77	72

Source: Best (1995).

an equal level of experience, job tenure, education, and hours of work. With community college graduates from the same year, a 3.5% gap was found in favour of males. When considering the general labour force in terms of earnings ratios based on hourly salary, in 1992 the female–male ratio was 0.79, which is significantly different than the ratio based on annual salaries (Coish and Hale 1994).

In interpreting the significance of these findings, several things must be kept in mind. First, the reason why women work fewer hours per week needs to be further examined. It is likely that unequal demands from private sphere duties are largely responsible for their lower availability for work. These findings suggest that, while systemic discrimination in the *workplace* against younger, more highly educated women is not a new problem, many women still appear to be subject to ideological pressures to remain anchored in the private sphere. And, the wage parity with males is partly the result of the declines in the salaries of men, including university-educated men. In fact, by 1993, university-educated men had about the same real earnings as men with high school diplomas in the late 1970s (Crompton 1996), while university-educated women gained over this period.

Table 4.5

Women as a Percentage of Full-Time
University Enrolment by Level and Year

Program/ Year	Under- graduate	Master's	Doctorate
1972–73	43	27	19
1981–82	50	41	31
1992–93	53	46	35

Source: Normand (1995).

In commenting on some of these findings, *Globe and Mail* columnist Margaret Wente wrote in 1995:

> It's not hard to guess why there's a difference in hours worked: Women have child-rearing and other obligations that compete heavily for their time. Some women's advocates cite this as proof of discrimination, as if all women would choose to work longer hours if only they didn't have to spend so much time cleaning house and looking after the gosh-darn kids. Economists prefer to cite "labour-supply decisions within the family context," which means that families tend to do the rational thing depending on their individual circumstances.

This is the crux of the problem we have been discussing. Women and men face material limitations in forming and maintaining families, and they utilize the resources available to them as best they can. They also base their decisions on what they have been taught to believe is right, which, for many, has been informed by the ideology of gender. Clearly, we are in a period where the greater involvement of women than men in the private sphere is a persistent phenomenon. While change is taking place, it is apparently very slow and it will likely take more time before equal involvement in these spheres becomes a reality.

Finally, women's participation in the higher educational system in Canada has shown dramatic increases in the past two decades. Between 1975 and 1990 there was a 79% increase in the number of full-time female university students, compared with a 15% increase for males. Table 4.5 shows enrolment increases from 1972 to 1993. By the early 1990s women made up more than half of university undergraduates, almost half of master's students, and a third of doctoral students. The lower rate of participation at the graduate levels is not well understood, but it probably reflects, in part, the same problems of integration of women into traditionally male-dominated fields, especially those that make great demands on one's time, such that private sphere commitments suffer. And, it is likely that many women are still channelled away from non-traditional fields though the processes of adolescence that affect their sense of identity and shape their career aspirations. But one long-term repercussion of the gender intensification process that may affect higher education and the adult workplace is the wedge driven between males and females as they are taught to define themselves "against" each other (i.e., in terms of masculinity versus femininity), making it difficult for them to cooperate as co-workers and colleagues.

Nonetheless, these changes in educational attainment suggest that impressive gains in social status have been made by women. It is noteworthy that it was the Canadian government, not corporations, that sponsored this investment in women's "human capital" (marketable skills), yet corporations benefit from trained labour paid for by taxpayers. Unfortunately, these gains for women come at a time when the corporate world is reorganizing itself and demanding even higher credentials for access to most corporate jobs. Thus, even though women now bring greater human capital with them to the labour force, the ante has been raised for everyone, so the returns may be less in the long run.

The Private Sphere

The history of industrial capitalism can be traced in the division of "men's work" and "women's work" into separate spheres. It is apparent that these spheres are reconverging in certain ways.

One index of activity in the private sphere is the amount of "unpaid work" done. Statistics Canada has been monitoring this for some time and has provided useful information regarding unpaid work done by men and women. A recent summary of this research revealed the following:

> In 1992, adult Canadians spent 25 billion hours on unpaid work. This represented 1,164 hours per adult, down from 1,223 hours in 1961. Women, on average, spent 78% more

time in 1992 on unpaid work than men did (1,482 hours per year, compared with 831 hours). They also spent 11% less time on unpaid work in 1992 than in 1961, though their participation in the labour force had nearly doubled over the same period. In contrast, men spent 6% more time on unpaid work. Nonetheless, women still did two-thirds of the unpaid work in 1992. *If paid and unpaid work were combined, women spent the same amount of time working as men did.* (Jackson 1996:26-27, emphasis added)

We can see from this that some progress has been made, although women have moved from one sphere to the other more than men. We can also see that, contrary to some views that present male–female relations as master–slave arrangements, when all labour is taken into account, men and women do the same amount. Thus, equal contributions are being made by men and women to the welfare of the community. The problem lies in sharing the labour in an equitable fashion — with women doing more paid labour and men doing more of the unpaid labour. Of course, properly rewarding unpaid labour by providing an income for it is a long-term goal that many support, but in the short term, we are not likely to see it, given the fiscal retrenchment taking place in Canada. According to Jackson (1996), unpaid labour represents about one-third of the Gross Domestic Product, or about $235 billion for 1992.

There is also evidence of greater sharing in the types of unpaid labour being done by men and women. Between the early 1960s and the 1990s men spent more time on meal preparation and clothing care, while women spent more time on transportation, volunteer work, and other out-of-home activities. It thus appears that the daily lives of many men and women have changed, and that more cooperation is taking place. However, women are still more likely to alter their employment patterns to accommodate responsibilities from the private sphere, especially when young children are involved.

One final indication of the extent of crossing over from one sphere to the other can be seen in the growth of dual-earner families. In a 1995 article in the journal *Perspectives on Labour and Income*, Susan Crompton and Lucy Geran described their increase as follows: "One of the most radical changes in Canadian society in the past 30 years has been the growth of dual-earner husband–wife families. Between 1967 and 1993, the proportion of such families almost doubled from 33% to 60%. In less than a generation, the traditional family with a breadwinning husband and a stay-at-home wife has been transformed into a new norm in which both spouses work outside the home" (1995:26).

One consequence of this greater involvement of married women in the workforce is that in an increasing number of families the wife earns more than the husband. In 1967 only 11% of wives earned more than their husbands. By 1993 this had more than doubled, to 25% (Crompton and Geran 1995). Moreover, the percentage of single-earner families in which the wife is the earner rose from 2% in 1967 to 20% in 1993. These trends accelerated in the early 1990s, as the fortunes of men in the workplace continued to deteriorate and those of women continued to improve. Again, dichotomous conceptions about the lives of contemporary men and women do not withstand the scrutiny of close inspection, supporting the notion of life-course convergence. Using gender to predict a life's course is becoming less accurate, as men and women face more equal odds of various fortunes and misfortunes.

Why Gender Inequality Is "Good" for Capitalism

We can now consider why progress towards equality has not been more satisfactory. Given that the material basis for a division of labour is no longer a factor and that the legitimacy of separating men and women into different spheres has been challenged, why do women not enjoy an equal share of the material resources of Canadian society, particularly in terms of equal pay and equal access to all jobs?

In public debate over this issue, especially in the media, the finger is often pointed at "men." The problem is often posed as simply one of men in general being sexist and unreasonable in their relations with women, or as "white males" being *the* source of the problems women face in seeking equality. While it is not difficult to find examples of such problems, such a generalization amounts to little more than stereotype, and it portrays women as passive, innocent and hapless victims of patriarchy. As discussed in the context of racialization in Chapter 3, stereotypes constitute errors of categorization in which members of a group are treated as if they were all the same. Stereotypes constitute the simplest and most primitive way of viewing the world, and they are usually wrong. And, stereotypes polarize men and women (or, e.g., blacks and whites). Polarization is often harmful to social reform movements because it divides those who have common interests and allows their opponents to prevail. If we are to achieve gender equality, both men and women must become involved as willing partners.

A materialist view helps to expose the self-defeating nature of anti-male (or anti-female) views. When social class is explicitly brought into the analysis, it becomes clear that not all men have better working conditions, higher pay, or more power than all women. There is no sexually defined master–slave relationship in Canadian society, contrary to some claims. In fact, the situation is far from absolute. On average, men do enjoy more of certain benefits than women, but it is also true that many of these benefits, such as wages, are decreasing for men and increasing for women. As we have seen among most recent university graduates, women are earning slightly more for their efforts than their male counterparts.

When we break down economic and social benefits by class, we see that stereotypical claims about gender inequalities are specious. For example, if we compare the average upper-class woman with the average working-class man, there is little merit to the notion that the poor man has anything over the rich woman. But even a less extreme comparison yields the same conclusion, as when middle-class professional women are compared with working-class men. In both cases, the women in question probably have far greater earning power, savings and self-esteem, personal worth, and more social power than the men. The women may in fact be the bosses of those men and therefore have legitimate authority over those men's lives and well-being. In such circumstances, it is hardly appropriate to say that affluent women are more oppressed by the system than are poor or working-class men.

With respect to the issue at hand — why gender inequalities are so persistent — our position is that these inequalities are, in part, perpetuated by anti-male stereotypes and by the more traditional stereotypes about women. As long as these prevail, men and women will be locked in struggles with each other in their day-to-day lives, blaming each other for their sense of injustice. The more individual men and women point their fingers at one another as the cause of their respective problems, the more the real sources of their problems go unnoticed. Thus, many contemporary women and men seem to have been duped by an old political ploy. This ploy — divide and conquer — has been used throughout history by those attempting to protect their interests. Simply stated, those with power first establish a perception of scarcity in an attempt to create divisions among those without power. It succeeds when those without power fight among themselves over the resources. The more the powerless fight each other, the less they will notice that the powerful enjoy a disproportionate share of community resources. Once this form of control is established, those in power simply have to provide enough "scraps" to keep the rest distracted by fighting with one another.

But why would capitalists be interested in perpetuating a "gender war" among individual women and men? Surely, it cannot matter that much to them, unless they derive personal gratification from it. Well, most probably do not. But if they are to maintain their superior position and lifestyle, they need a capitalist economy that is maximally effective. And, the basic principle of capital accumulation is the extraction of profit from the labour of others; the lower the wages, the greater the profit. Thus, inequality is an essential condition of capitalism — wages have to be kept as low as possible to maximize profit. And just like racism, sexism is a proven method for doing just that.

Of course, few people would choose to work for low wages if they had the opportunity to receive higher ones, especially for doing the same job. Accordingly, capitalists have found it convenient to recruit cheap labour based on existing prejudices and stereotypes. In this case, the typical example taken from late-modern society is the legacy of patriarchy and the ideology of gender. Capitalists, both male and female, have played upon people's stereotypes about a "differentness" between men and women. In playing on these ideas, and convincing people of them (with varying degrees of success), capitalists have succeeded in maintaining wage disparities and job segregation — getting women to work for lower wages in low-skilled jobs. (Interestingly, to the extent that the struggle against this exploitation has been successful, capitalists have turned to another segment of the population — young people — for cheap labour, as we will see in the next chapter.)

Throughout the history of industrial capitalism, the capitalist class's superior position has been subsidized by women's free labour in the household. Without this free labour, that is, if capitalists had to pay their fair share of the costs of bearing and raising the children who become their workers, their accumulation of profits would have been much less over this whole period. Little wonder, then, that the media and institutions controlled or influenced by the capitalist class have sustained stereotypes about women and men and nurtured the ideology of gender.

In addition to having reserve armies of cheap or free labour, capitalists have also found markets for their goods and services in a "genderized" society. Thus, capitalists have a vested interest in maintaining a basic division between men and women in terms of their very "essence." The more men and women are convinced that they are different "species," the more they can be sold special products and services. (Note in this context the popularity of John Gray's (1992) best-selling pop-psychology book, *Men Are from Mars, Women Are from Venus.*) Marketers know very well that "gendering" products works, because much of the population has a well-developed set of gender stereotypes about themselves and others. Much of this marketing plays on heterosexual attraction, with women and men sold billions of dollars in products and services that ostensibly give them the inside track in attracting desirable mates. And so men and women are not only alienated from their sexuality as it might otherwise manifest itself, but women are set in competition with each other in trying to look most "attractive" according to arbitrary and unrealistic standards set by marketers. These influences now begin in childhood, become intensified in adolescence, and continue into adulthood. While individual women and men might resist and escape these influences, they are nonetheless potent cultural forces not easily undone. Consequently, many individual lives are deeply affected, including those of young women who invest more in their appearance than in their inner selves and personal potential, with predictable consequences in later life (for instance, being unprepared for non-traditional jobs, or for being widowed or divorced).

The commodification of women's and men's sexuality extends to the literal selling of women's and men's bodies through pornography and various forms of exotic dancing bordering on prostitution. These multi-billion-dollar industries draw women in particular from various walks of life, encouraging them to rationalize their involvement as a natural extension of the sexual displays they have been taught to view as "normal." Many women become involved in these industries to "make ends meet," generally because of limited job opportunities and low pay elsewhere. Some need to put themselves through college or university, while some single mothers become involved in these activities to give their children more material benefits.

Conclusion

Our examination of the history of the gendered division of labour in terms of its material basis suggests that pioneering European men

and women worked together, sharing the same paramount goal —
survival. In the earliest days of pioneer settlement, there were no
"middle class" careers to compete for; indeed, there was little in the
way of paid labour, and there were also few products to be purchased.
Most of what was consumed was made by the family in the home or
grown in the surrounding fields. By most accounts, women enjoyed
a much higher status in this preindustrial setting than they did during
the industrial era, when men were drawn into the paid-labour force
and women were relegated to home and unpaid labour. Paid labour
carried with it higher status, and money bought privilege. Men's
status increased, particularly for those who became part of the so-
called middle and upper middle classes, while women's status decreased because their labour was no longer seen as an essential and
valid contribution to the economy. Moreover, the change in the status
of children and teenagers further affected the status of women. As
children were increasingly viewed as "innocents" to be protected and
educated, they were expected to contribute less and less to household
maintenance, so the menial labour they once performed was largely
taken up by their mothers.

When the central goal is survival, there is not much need for
elaborate ideologies to justify one's role in the division of labour.
Hence, most pioneering Canadian men and women probably believed
the roles they were allocated were legitimate, as they often worked
together in the same sphere. Today, however, there is no justification
for the segregation into separate spheres that occurred during the
early industrial period, yet, because of the persistence of the ideology
of gender, many people continue to believe there is. The persistence
of this belief is perhaps one reason why men and women are so
divided — they see little higher order basis for cooperation. Instead,
many see each other as competitors for a different kind of survival
— well-paid jobs that provide personal comforts as well as self-esteem and self-actualization.

Thus, we find men and women of the 1990s as somewhat opposed
groups in competition with each other over the scarce resources of
the workplace. Women's move into the workplace would perhaps
have been smoother if not for the recessions of the 1980s and early
1990s, and for corporate restructuring. With downsizing, outsour-
cing, and contracting out, more and more men and women are scram-
bling to maintain an income. The fact that they are facing each other
in line-ups for these jobs has not helped create an atmosphere of
cooperation and common interest. It is not the individual men in these

job line-ups who are responsible for the recessions and the corporate restructuring, yet the politics of resentment between men and women is often played out at this interpersonal level. Both men and women have a common interest in escaping their precarious situations, in finding jobs that pay well and have reasonable security, pleasant working conditions, and employers who value them. However, the more individual men and women blame each other for not having their own interests met in these ways, the more corporate interests can continue their practice of reaping profits at the expense of those who have nothing to bargain with but their labour.

Within this context, we can better understand the current "adjustment problems" in Western societies regarding the integration of women into the paid-labour force. This public sphere has been dominated by men and has been structured to suit their interests. Women attempting to move into this sphere have encountered prejudices and practices that make them feel unwelcome and even physically threatened. Efforts to deal with these problems have also met resistance, as one can see on nightly newscasts that feature stories about employment equity, sexual harassment, and workplace restructuring to accommodate daycare and parental leave.

When the circumstances individual women and men currently face are viewed in the context of capitalism, two things become apparent. The first is the inevitability of continued inequality under capitalism: until capitalists find other groups to exploit (and they have now turned to youth, as we see in the next chapter) women (and racialized ethnic minorities) will continue to be targeted by class or economic and ideological forces. The second is that the gains that have been made towards equality have not threatened the entrenched interests of capital. As much as the various waves of feminism have brought attention to women's issues, change has only occurred in those areas that do not directly affect the accumulation of capital among the bourgeoisie (e.g., equity in higher education). Indeed, unless the material conditions are conducive to it, little real change seems to take place, which helps explain why some countries have improved levels of gender equality without a feminist movement.

An important lesson emerges from this analysis: single-issue approaches to social justice (like "women's issues") are likely to achieve limited success if they are divorced from materialist, class issues. Indeed, since all women are not the same and are not likely to have the same interests, any talk of "women's interests" pure and simple is bound to create difficulty: because women have multiple identities, then, there is no logical reason why gender or social position based on attributes of gender should be uniformly assumed to override class, ethnic, or other identities that may divide women. Rather, the idea is to identify "gender interests," both practical and strategic.

Strategic gender interests are feminist interests and speak to the theoretical and philosophical concepts behind such things as sexual subordination and inequality, abortion rights, and the right to be free from physical violence and sexual assault. Practical gender interests are more concrete and issue specific. Given the place that women traditionally occupy in the gendered division of labour, these may include mobilization around the need for daycare, for school bus service, or for the efficient delivery of water and electricity to rural homes. And the organization of women around practical gender issues must be linked to organization around strategic gender interests (Allahar 1995b:66-67) and be articulated with issues of class, race, ethnicity, and national identity that challenge the subordination of women (Acosta-Belén and Bose 1990:314).

Care must be taken, however, to ensure that gender issues, whether strategic or practical, are not manipulated by opportunistic gender entrepreneurs who have other agendas, and who might seek to employ the "divide and conquer" strategy that pits women against men as a smoke screen. This is not to say, though, that the single issues are not themselves worthy of attention. But without a sense of the "big picture" they can cause divisions among the very people who ought to work together towards common interests or who might be genuinely united around concerns for social justice. Thus, rather than addressing issues such as the inherent demand of capitalism for unequal income distribution, progressive women often fight with progressive men over scarce resources. And, progressive or not, many women are led to believe that their salvation lies simply in wage parity with men, even though most men's salaries have decreased in the past two decades, rather than over more general issues of social justice, which can only be effectively pursued by a unified movement of both women and men.

5

The Disenfranchisement of Youth

In contrast to the widespread concern over racial and gender inequalities during the 1980s and 1990s, attention to intergenerational inequalities has been relatively muted. Even among those most affected — young people themselves — there seems to be a lack of widespread, *genuine* interest in understanding what lies behind growing inequities among the different age groups. We encountered this in 1994 when we released *Generation on Hold*. We even encountered a curious form of denial among some of our sociology colleagues, who are supposed to be attuned to social issues. Certainly there is disaffection among some young people and concern among some adults, but it seems often to be poorly informed and diffusely directed. The problem seems to be that many people still prefer individualistic over structural explanations of inequalities.

Within this context of relative indifference and misdirected explanations, we offer a review and analysis of intergenerational relations that we hope will help young people recognize some of their common interests. In doing so, we hope to help them better understand their life chances and relations with other age groups. In contrast to most treatments of age inequality, our focus is on the young rather than the elderly. It is not that the elderly are without their problems, but in Canada the fortunes of the elderly have increased over the past 20 years proportionately to the declining fortunes of the young. Moreover, estimates of the standard of living of the elderly are often based on income, which lead to underestimates, given the accumulated equity of many older individuals.

What we offer here is a refinement and update of what we wrote in *Generation on Hold*, since the circumstances many young people face have not improved. In fact, the most recent studies (from the mid-1990s) suggest that certain conditions have continued to deteriorate.

There is another difference between our discussion of gender inequality in the last chapter and our discussion of intergenerational inequality here. The history of gender inequality reveals a story of lost status for women with the advent of industrialization, and of progress made as industrialization has moved into its more advanced stages. There was an optimistic tone of something "lost, then found." The history of age inequality, however, suggests a somewhat different story. Youth in Canadian society "found" more equality with industrialization because of the value placed on their labour. (This particularly applied to young men and young unmarried women.) But, especially in the past two decades, this has eroded. So, there is here more of a pessimistic tone of something "found and lost."

The issue of gender may be raised in terms of whether the experiences of young women are markedly different from those of young men. Should we really have separate chapters dealing with each sex? From our research, however, it is clear that young men and young women increasingly share more with their age-mates than they do with older same-sex persons. For example, we traced in the last chapter a convergence in educational experiences and earning power among young men and women. In the late twentieth century, the *commonality of youth* binds them together, probably more so than in any period in the past. The movement towards gender-role equality seems to be largely responsible for this, as we find young men and women increasingly working, studying, and playing together far more than in the past. Thus, the differences among the inequality issues we examine below are now one of degree rather than kind. This said, it is apparent that young men and women are still affected differently by segregation in the workplace, and their socialization experiences also differ when it comes to matters like femininity and masculinity.

Class enters our analysis in our observations of the ways in which young people have been economically disenfranchised. Many young people are downwardly mobile within their class of origin. And, for many of them, aspirations to membership in the new middle class have been thwarted. Certainly, upward mobility out of the working class now seems increasingly rare, and is unlikely in the future, except for a few exceptional cases. There is little doubt that poverty is increasing among young people, and the future does not look bright for those now growing up. It is likely that a sizeable number of young people will not be able to work their way out of poverty, now or in the future.

Division of Labour by Age

In addition to the class-, ethnic-, and gender-based divisions of labour, societies also divide tasks on an age basis — and with even more variation. Generally, pre-or non-industrial societies assign children the simpler, more menial tasks (and these tasks are often divided again according to gender). As an individual ages, the tasks often become more complex, often less menial, and the rewards normally increase; but so too do the responsibilities.

In the previous chapter we argued that those who are recognized as making a direct contribution to the welfare of the community tend to have relatively higher status. When we examine the history of age relations in Canada, we find marked changes: in recent years the young are losing ground in terms of being welcomed into the workplace and attaining the independence of adulthood.

These losses have both material and ideological bases, but before reviewing these it is useful to examine the commonsense idea of "starting at the bottom." Societies generally give children the most basic and menial tasks, but as they grow, the tasks often become more complex and carry greater responsibility. "Starting at the bottom" implies that there is somewhere upwards to move to. In industrial societies this has meant that one can work up the "ladder of success." As we see, this basic assumption has been challenged in many modern workplaces, as many young people now start at the bottom — and stay there. Young women, recent immigrants, and members of certain races have been accustomed to this for some time, but now it increasingly applies to young men of European descent, too. Given that the labour force was once dominated by young men, this constitutes a major cultural change over the past century.

Age Stratification in Canada

What has happened in Canadian history to produce this deterioration in the life chances of the young and the increasing disparities between youth and adult opportunities? To answer this question we will examine underlying changes in material and ideological conditions. First, we will examine how changes in material conditions have affected three institutions associated with the transition to adulthood — the workplace, education, and the family; then we will speculate about the ideological conditions that have emerged to complement these changes.

Changing Material Conditions

Two sets of material conditions associated with the rise of industrial capitalism appear to have had dramatic influences on youth–adult relations over the past century, to the detriment of young people: (1) changing demographic patterns and (2) changing means of production.

Changing Demographic Patterns and the Competition Ratio

In the last chapter we described changes in the life experiences of the average Canadian woman and man over the past three centuries. Particularly striking is the increase in life expectancy, from about 30 to 35 years in the early 1700s to about 75 to 80 today. In the earliest colonial days, there was very little paid labour, as the vast majority of work involved subsistence agriculture and the household production of basic goods. Accordingly, most men and women worked the land and produced most of their own essentials. Even at the turn of the twentieth century, about 65% of the population lived in rural areas, and some 40% of the population was still engaged in agricultural labour. At that time about 45% of the labour force was still employed in the primary sector, about 27% was in the secondary sector, and only 28% was in the tertiary sector. By 1990, however, the percentage employed in the primary sector had dropped to only 6%, while the secondary sector remained relatively stable at 23%, and a full 71% were now employed in the tertiary sector (McDonald and Chen 1993). The *wage* labour force of the eighteenth and nineteenth centuries was made up mainly of *young* males, who worked on average only about two decades before they died.

In the twentieth century an increasing proportion of the population has lived well beyond what we now call young adulthood. This "aging population" has influenced intergenerational competition for scarce resources, particularly workplace resources. The competition between younger and older age groups can be be referred to as the "competition ratio," because it can be expressed statistically. As Table 5.1 shows, in both 1861 and 1881, those in the range of 15 to 29 years of age outnumbered those in the wider range of 30 to 64 years. Expressed as a ratio, there was slightly more than one potential young worker for every older worker. When we look at changes in this ratio over the following century, we find it dropping steadily (with the exception of the 1981 figures). By 1991 there was a competition ratio of about one to two. In other words, there are now *twice* as many older people as younger people who are potential competi-

Table 5.1

The Competition Ratio:
The Changing Proportion of Adult Age Groups
Between 1861 and 1991

	Age groups		Ratio of age groups	
	15–29	30–64	15–29 30–64	Median age of the
	Male/Female (000)	Male/Female (000)	Male/Female	popu- lation
1861	368/358	333/292	1.11/1.23	17.8
1881	667/674	612/558	1.10/1.21	20.1
1901	754/731	899/830	.84/.88	22.7
1921	1,102/1,098	1,649/1,450	.67/.76	23.9
1941	1,543/1,515	2,347/2,135	.66/.71	27.0
1961	1,945/1,911	3,433/3,365	.57/.57	26.5
1981	3,441/3,396	4,806/4,859	.72/.70	29.6
1991	3,126/3,080	6,081/6,147	.51/.50	33.5

Sources: Bureau of Agriculture and Statistics, Census Dept. (1863) — estimates are for Upper Canada and Lower Canada; Department of Agriculture (1884); The Census Office (1906); Department of Trade & Commerce (1925); Dominion Bureau of Statistics (1946); Dominion Bureau of Statistics (1962); Statistics Canada (1982); Statistics Canada (1992). Ratios calculated by the authors. Median ages for 1881 to 1991 are from McVey and Kalbach (1995). The median age for 1861 was calculated by the authors from Leacy (1983). Note that Easterlin (1978:422) found similar ratios for the American male population, as follows: 1920 = .667, 1940 = .630, 1960 = .502, 1980 = .721, and 1990 = .546 (the latter two are his projections from the late 1970s).

tors in the workplace. It should also be noted that in the 1800s many older people would not have been as physically able as the young to work in the primary or secondary sectors that provided most of the paid labour. Now, owing to computers, technological advances, and improvements in health care, older workers are more physically suited to the modern workplace dominated by the lighter tertiary sector. And so the competition now may be even greater than the proportions alone suggest.

A consequence of these patterns is that the economic appeal of young people as workers has almost certainly decreased dramatically over time. Today, a much larger proportion of older people are available and willing to engage in paid labour than ever before. The impact of this development in the 1990s has become increasingly obvious, as many older workers affected by corporate restructuring have been forced to take jobs normally performed by younger workers. This is, in part, due to the fact that in the past corporations were usually structured as pyramids. However, changing demographic patterns have meant that as larger numbers of young people have tried to move up this corporate structure in the late twentieth century, many have found themselves blocked. As David Foot noted in his 1996 book, *Boom, Bust and Echo: How to Profit From the Coming Demographic Shift*: "We have been trying to promote a rectangle [large numbers of young people] up a triangle, and it can't be done. This system only works when there are more younger than older employees, which was exactly the case over most of the twentieth century as the modern corporation took shape."

With many of the lower and middle level jobs taken by older workers, an increasing number of young people seeking a foothold in the labour market cannot find the job they want. Many are forced into the lowest subordinate positions, which are part-time, low paying, and provide little opportunity for advancement — "McJobs." Others are unsuccessful and become "discouraged workers" who stop looking for work altogether and therefore do not show up in the official statistics. When the number of discouraged workers is added to the number of officially unemployed, the resulting unemployment rate is about 50% higher than the official one.

These developments seem to have had a dramatic impact on the life experiences of young males. As noted, in the 1800s this group dominated the workplace. They now have to compete with twice as many males over 30, and also with a growing proportion of females looking for work. Thus, in 1991 the competition ratio for young males was nearer to one-to-five than the one-to-one of a century ago. To the extent that some young men predicate their identity on the role of "good provider," we can see a potential source of conflict, and perhaps resentment, for them.

The life experiences of young women have also changed dramatically but for somewhat different reasons. They increasingly participate in the public sphere in parallel with young men. In fact, young Canadian women and men now share certain life experiences to an unprecedented extent (cf. D. Anderson 1991). Their rate of participation in the educational system is an obvious example, but so too is their rate of participation in the workforce. This means that, along with problems unique to them, young women also face most of the same problems young males do when trying to enter the public sphere. Accordingly, as age inequalities have grown and gender inequalities have lessened, young women have had an increasing amount in common with younger men rather than with older women.

Clearly, then, these demographic shifts have contributed to changes in the lives of average Canadians, both female and male. The transition to adulthood has altered as the period of pre-adult dependency has increased. This process began when adolescence (the teen years) became a prolongation of childhood dependency; more recently, the period of young adulthood (the twenties) has taken on characteristics of adolescent dependency. In fact, the Canadian Youth Foundation called in 1995 for the Canadian government to officially recognize that the period of youth be extended to age 29, because the "definition of youth used by the government ... is not an accurate reflection of the ages young people are leaving school and beginning careers." This call was an effort to direct employment-policy initiatives *beyond* the 15 to 24 age group. The foundation's reasoning was that unemployed people between 25 and 29 are different from younger unemployed people only in that they have been unemployed longer.

Technological Displacement

The decreasing economic value of young workers and the competition they face in the workforce have been exacerbated by changes in the technologies used in producing goods and services. Throughout this century, techniques of mass production have been refined by owners and managers of capital intent on increasing profit. The increase in profit has been made possible largely by replacing workers with machines: in the secondary sector, robots continue to replace factory workers; in the service sector, computers continue to replace lower and middle managers, clerical workers, and various other workers. These trends have tended to carve the middle out of the labour force, leaving the highest and lowest paid workers in greatest demand. Foot (1996:68–9) summarized the problem in *Boom, Bust and Echo*:

As recently as the early 1980s, it was cheaper to add workers than to add machines. But by the 1990s, the cost of labour in Canada was twice the cost of machines ... So today's companies are adding machines instead of labour. The result is improved productivity but increased unemployment. The conventional wisdom in the 1980s was that technology would eventually create as many jobs as it took. Although the jury is still out on this question, the optimistic view is increasingly being called into question. Technology continues, at a relentless pace, to destroy far more jobs than it creates.

Whatever the future might hold, it appears that change in age group ratios and technological displacement have now dovetailed to devalue the bargaining power of young workers. In spite of being the most educated generation in Canadian history, many young workers find themselves unable to get even a foothold in the workforce, let alone to pursue the types of careers their educators and parents told them constitute the basis of happiness and success. As David Foot noted, the "unskilled entry-level jobs leading to middle-class security no longer exist. That is why the labour force participation rate for people between 15 and 24 fell to a 19-year low in 1995."

Institutional Changes over the Twentieth Century

To help us understand the impact of these changing material conditions, it is useful to trace what has happened to those in their teens and twenties over the past century. Of course, there are variations among individuals, by age, gender, race, and class, and two world wars and a depression affected these patterns. However, a comparison of the beginning and the end of the century gives us a useful historical perspective.

We begin with a thumbnail sketch: Around 1900, only a small number of teens attended secondary schools. Almost half were involved in agricultural labour, while the rest were employed in paid labour, often making a living wage, or close to it. Many lived with their families and were able to make considerable financial contributions to the family.

As we approach the year 2000, the vast majority of teens attend secondary schools, and over 60% of secondary school graduates go directly to post-secondary institutions. However, less than one-third of those aged 18 to 24 are employed and sufficiently well paid to afford them independence from their parents. Those who stay at home rarely contribute much financially and usually make only minor contributions to household labour (although young females do more housework than young males). Their parents often subsidize them with free or cheap room and board, or allowances, and mothers often provide "domestic" services for them.

Three institutions — the workplace, the education system, and the family — have affected the experiences and life chances of young people in the twentieth century. We will now give attention to each of them in their order of importance as factors in bringing about the current situation.

The Workplace

Those groups recognized as making a direct productive contribution to the welfare of the community tend to have higher status in any society. This principle is based on observations of non-capitalist societies. In capitalist societies, it does not hold for the parasitic capitalists, movie and sports heroes, and others who are able to take advantage of the system to reap extraordinary benefits without producing anything of tangible value.

When we look at key indicators of direct productive contribution — wages, employment levels, types of jobs held — we see that, as a group, young people have lost much of their ability to make such contributions relative to other age groups. Indeed, the above-mentioned changes in material conditions have dramatically affected the share of resources young people are allotted from the collective resource pool.

DECLINING WAGES

When we examine changes in wages over the past 25 years we find a steady and significant redistribution of wealth by age. In the 1960s males aged 16 to 24 earned incomes that were about on par with those over 24, depending on the job. Picot and Myles (1996:17) show how the various age groups in Canada began at more or less the same wage level in 1969, but have since steadily differentiated. By 1993 the 17 through 24 age group was only making about 5% more than it did in 1969, while the oldest age groups were making about 30% more. Adjusting for inflation, those in the 17 through 24 age group declined about 19% in real annual earnings, while those aged 25 through 34 fell 10%.

These trends are illustrated in Table 5.2, where we can see the age-based redistribution of income in Canada from 1981 to 1991.

Table 5.2

Change in Average Income, 1981–1991, Adjusting for Inflation, by Age (%)

	Age cohort						
	<25	25–34	35–44	45–54	55–64	>65	All ages
Families	-20.7	-4.9	0	6.1	4.3	14.9	3.5
Unattached individuals	-21.7	-13.2	-8.4	3.8	4.8	12.4	-0.8

Source: adapted from Ross and Shillington (1994).

These figures suggest that, contrary to the image the media often provide, what is taking place seems to be more than a simple competition for resources between the so-called baby boomers and baby busters. Rather, redistribution of income is more continuous along age lines. Over the decade, economic benefits accrued to those over 45, but in 1991 the early baby boomers were just reaching age 45. Thus, contrary to public perception, the early baby boomers (aged 35–44) actually suffered losses in the 1980s. Later baby boomers (aged 25–34) suffered even more. However, neither group was hit as hard as the so-called baby bust aged 25 and younger. It is telling that those who made gains during this period were the very ones making the bulk of the decisions about such things as wages and benefits (i.e., those 45 and over — the pre-baby boomers). A 1993 Statistics Canada report made this observation: "In the face of downward wage pressures from globalization, older workers are better able to immunize themselves from growing wage competition as a result of seniority rules, firm-specific training and other 'institutional' barriers that favour job incumbents over new labour market entrants."

Most current studies from the mid-1990s show that these trends have continued. The downward trend in wages and employment prospects continues for young men, regardless of whether they have high school or university educations. In contrast, wages and employment prospects continue to fall only for young women with high school educations, especially those aged 24 and under. Crompton (1996) found that men and women aged between 25 and 29 with high school diplomas saw their wages decline between 1979 and 1993 (as much as 17% for men). Moreover, by 1993, university-educated men in this age group earned about the same in real terms as did men of the same age with high school diplomas in the late 1970s. University-educated women made gains over the same period, and by 1990 were actualy making more "than their male counterparts [with equivalent] experience, job tenure, education and hours of work" (Wannell and Caron 1994:ii). Note, however, that the wage gap closed in part because of declining earnings among males.

According to a 1994 Statistics Canada analysis, there is little evidence that this is a temporary stage in a cycle of increase and decline. Wages for both young men and women have dropped "within all educational levels … within all major industrial groups … and all occupational categories." Accordingly, the drop in earnings cannot be simply attributed to the increase in subordinate service work taken up by young workers or to business cycles.

This redistribution of income was not merely the result of certain isolated individuals feathering their own nests, or those of their age mates. Indeed, many of the policy adjustments undertaken by the Canadian state have made government a key mediator between the interests of capital and young workers. One such policy is the setting of minimum wage levels. In the mid-1970s, the minimum wage would put a person about 40% *above* the official poverty line; now it puts a person 30% *below* that line. Notably, two-thirds of minimum wage earners are under 24 years of age. Here, government policies have clearly contributed to age-based discrimination. Few people seem to be aware of the role the state has played in mediating the interests of capital in this regard, and many of those who are aware seem to see nothing wrong with it.

DECLINING WORKFORCE PARTICIPATION

Not only are the youngest being hardest hit in their earning power, but their opportunities for any jobs at all have diminished. Between 1989 and 1994, while other age groups maintained their participation rates in the workforce, the participation rate of the young dropped dramatically from 71% to 62%. This decline accounted for an overall drop in the unemployment rate at the time — to 9.7%. Of the G7 countries, in 1993, Canada had the third highest youth unemployment rate (about 17%), lower than only France (about 25%) and Italy (about 30%).

What actually happened was that many would-be workers went "missing" from official statistics; otherwise the unemployment rate would have been 13%. Between 1989 and 1994 some 300,000 young Canadians simply gave up trying to find work; as a result, they were no longer counted as unemployed. Granted, many of these discouraged workers went back to school, but, as we see below, this often involves a fruitless scramble for credentials in a job market characterized by extensive underemployment of graduates with higher education. Interestingly, Statistics Canada's 1994 analysis argued that the drop in workforce participation might have been greater if it were not for the lower wages young people now make. In other words, their extremely low wages seem to have enhanced their employability in some sectors (Betcherman and Morissette 1994).

Recently women over 25 have made the most gains in employment — presumably in response to employment equity initiatives. Although they constituted 38% of the workforce, they found 52% of the jobs since 1990, while men over 25 found jobs in proportion to their representation in the population.

JOB GHETTOIZATION

Young workers not only are paid less and participate in the workforce less, they are also becoming less well represented in all job categories except consumer services. Indeed, it is in the subordinate service occupations that their (cheap) labour is most in demand.

Betcherman and Morissette tell us that between 1981 and 1989, the proportion of service sector jobs held by young workers aged 16 to 24 rose from 69.7% to 75.8%, while in the goods sector it dropped from 30.3% to 24.2%. The two most common service sector jobs held in 1989 were retail trade (22.7%) and accommodation and food (13.7%). Statistics Canada (ibid) noted from these trends a "substantial absolute decline of youth employment in the goods sector and in public administration, health, social services, and education" and concluded that for "earlier generations of young people, these industries typically offered good entry-level opportunities." When broken down by gender, over 84% of employed females between the ages of 15 and 19 worked in the service sector, compared with about 60% of their male counterparts.

A clear picture emerges here: the jobs available to the young are increasingly unskilled, poorly paid, subordinate dead-end jobs, with little chance for advancement. At the same time, these are also the most common jobs available. Two-thirds of the new jobs created in the Canadian labour force are in sales and service, suggesting a long-term trend that many young people will be confronted with throughout their working lives.

Higher Education and the Credentials Paradox

In the workplace of the 1990s a person without higher education faces severely limited economic prospects. The unemployment rate of young people without post-secondary credentials is about three times higher than for those with them (Canadian Youth Foundation 1995). And those without a post-secondary degree are less employable in most sectors of the economy. Moreover, a university education is a good investment in salary level and future earning power. According to Statistics Canada, nearly two-thirds of new jobs between 1991 and 2000 are going to require at least 13 years of education or training, and 45% of them will require more than 16 years.

Male university graduates earn about 60% more than those with high school or less. In the United States, the overall salary difference is 77% between university and high school graduates. In Canada, female university graduates earn about twice as much as do women with high school or less, up significantly from a differential of 71% in 1984. The lifetime payback for a university education can be sizeable. Spread over 40 years, it could amount to an average of $600,000 in 1990 dollars (Fournier, Butlin and Giles 1994; Association of Universities and Colleges in Canada 1996).

However, many highly educated workers, especially those with non-technical degrees, perform tasks that have little to do with their formal education. But without the credentials, employability and earning power are seriously jeopardized. To understand this paradox, we need to have a sense of the history of the educational system.

The primary and secondary educational systems in Canada emerged, in part, to provide daily structure to young people displaced by the increasing technologization of agriculture and manufacturing. Primary school enrolment in the nineteenth century was low and sporadic. Many parents were not supportive of compulsory education, and it was difficult to get children to attend school regularly. Even by 1901, although efforts to implement compulsory education had been under way for two decades in many provinces, the average daily attendance in primary schools was only 62%, and the typical student received only about six years of schooling (Phillips 1957).

It was not until several decades into this century that enrolments increased to the point where the educational system began to take its current form as the major institution governing the lives of young Canadians. In Ontario, for example, although the population doubled between 1900 and 1950, enrolments in secondary schools increased sixfold. From Table 5.3 we can see that in the 1920s about 25% of

Table 5.3

Percentage of Young Men and Women Attending School, 1921–1991

	Ages 15–19		Ages 20–24	
	Men	Women	Men	Women
1921	23	27	3	2
1931	32	35	4	2
1941	34	37	5	3
1951	41	40	7	3
1961	62	56	12	5
1971	74	56	12	5
1981	66	66	21	16
1991	79	80	32	33

Source: adapted from Normand (1995).

those aged 15 to 19 attended school, but by 1991 80% did. Of those aged 20 to 24, only about 3% attended in 1921, but by 1991 about one-third did. In fact, this latter age group increased their participation almost threefold in the 1980s.

Currently, Canada has one of the highest participation rates and most expensive publicly funded educational systems in the world. Nobert and McDowell (1994) reported that current expenditures on post-secondary education are 21 times higher than they were at the beginning of the 1950s, totalling about 15 billion dollars in 1991–2. Of the OECD countries, Canada puts the greatest share of its public expenditures into post-secondary education (4.6%). Canada has the second highest post-secondary participation rate in the world, second to the United States (both countries have about twice the participation rate of other developed countries). Taking the entire population, 17% of Canadians have studied at university (compared with 24% in the United States).

On the face of it, this looks like an enviable achievement that less developed countries should emulate. Nevertheless, there is more to this picture than simple enrolment figures.

Let us not be misunderstood here. It is admirable that Canada has tried to educate its citizens to such an extent. Given the choice, most societies would surely prefer formally educated citizens to under-educated ones. There are clear benefits to having an educated population, and it is a laudable democratic ideal to try to reach as many people as possible. However, an unintended consequence of Canada's mass-education system places many graduates in a labour market that does not need the skills it has taught them.

The roots of the problem can be found in the 1960s, when the higher education system was expanded dramatically and many new community colleges and universities were built. This expansion led to a ninefold increase in post-secondary enrolment between 1950 and 1990. The assumption was that the skills transmitted through higher education — human capital — would meet the needs of an advanced industrial economy and generate economic wealth for both the individual graduate and for the society as a whole. This human capital assumption has been borne out to some extent, but is not a full explanation of educational outcomes.

But by the mid-1970s, graduate underemployment was visibly becoming a widespread problem. Stories about graduates with PhDs driving taxis abounded in the media. This came about because the public sector had reached its capacity to absorb university graduates while the number of people with higher degrees continued to grow. Without ongoing expansion in the public sector, graduates increasingly turned to the private sector. Although there were "good jobs" to be found in business and professional services, many found only "bad jobs" in consumer services. As the supply of graduates grew, a buyers' market in favour of employers developed in most sectors. Employers could take those with the highest credentials, even for lower skill jobs, so many of those with higher degrees found themselves taking jobs that did not require any or all of their skills. Consequently, those *without* higher degrees faced increasingly stiff competition for (any) jobs.

By the late 1980s almost one-half of community college graduates and over 40% of those with BAs found themselves underemployed, doing jobs that did not require an advanced credential (Nobert, McDowell and Goulet 1992). This applied especially to non-technical, liberal arts degrees. Faced with this, many chose to seek further credentials to get ahead of the pack (and would then have been counted as among the "discouraged workers" mentioned above). In the late 1980s many people were in a scramble for credentials, trying to gain some advantage to enhance career possibilities, and as many as 50% of community college and university graduates were re-en-rolling in subsequent educational programs. With an oversupply of higher degrees, workplace demand for many of them decreased, so higher educational graduates had less to bargain with because their credentials had lost market value.

The market value of many credentials has continued to fall from the 1970s as more and more people obtained higher degrees. This process accelerated in the 1980s when higher educational enrolments in Canada increased by some 40%. It was not until 1992 that the rate of growth began to decline, and not until 1995 that there was actually a decline — of 1% — in university enrolments (Association of Universities and Colleges in Canada 1996).

Now, at the end of the twentieth century, the educational system has become perhaps the most important institution regulating what has become a prolonged period of adolescence and youth. Its role has become even more apparent over the past 20 years, as increasing numbers of graduates have encountered diminished job opportunities and returned to school, only to find themselves caught up in the scramble for credentials. Consequently, the stakes are now higher for everyone, making many years of expensive education necessary if one hopes to have an interesting career and a decent salary.

The Family and Safety Net Parents

In Canada about two-thirds of unmarried people in their early twenties, and one-third of those in their late twenties, live with their parents. American data reveal the same trend. In fact, this has become a trend in most developed countries (cf. Jones 1994). In Italy, according to D'Emilio (1995), some 50% of males aged 25 to 34 live with one or both parents, apparently taking advantage of free domestic services and parental permissiveness regarding sexual privacy. Concern for this was expressed recently in an ad in which stay-at-home males were referred to as *mammoni* (mama's boys). The ads read "*Ancora a casa da mamma?*" ("Still living at home with mama?") with a picture of an adult male dressed like a baby. Italy has the highest youth unemployment rate among the G7 countries, as well as the highest ratio of youth unemployment to total unemployment — three to one.

The trend, which continued upward through the late 1970s and early 1980s, seems to have stabilized in the 1990s. This increased dependency of young Canadians on their parents is of concern, but the stabilization may mean that the trend has plateaued. It is possible that a saturation point has been reached: perhaps contemporary families simply cannot absorb any more young adults. Some families may not be able to maintain their adult children because of their own economic problems, while other families cannot for emotional reasons. Interpersonal conflicts can be a problem, especially if both biological parents are no longer residing in the same home.

This pattern is reminiscent of arrangements early in the century when proportionately as many, or more, young people lived in their parents' home. But they did so for a variety of reasons, including mutual survival and support, which were especially important before the advent of social assistance programs. Such arrangements seem to have been more to the *collective* benefit of the family as a whole, to which the young person made different kinds of valuable contributions. These arrangements were not necessarily a sign of lower status in the wider society for the young person involved, but rather one of kin obligation, especially for young women. In contrast, living with parents now seems to be more often a "safety net" for young people, marginal in the workplace and unable to afford independent living.

When we take a longer view, even broader trends emerge. Current living arrangements appear quite different from those that prevailed in mid-nineteenth-century Canada. For example, in Hamilton, Ontario, in 1851, only about 20% of males and females in their early twenties lived in their parents' homes. Instead, boarding was a common living arrangement. In the early twentieth century most young working-class people, both male and female, went to work in their early teens and contributed about half of their income to their parents' household. Some young men could actually make more than their fathers, or when several children were working, their joint income could be greater than the father's income. This period spent living with working offspring was sometimes the most prosperous time in the parents' lives, and the offspring's status in the family benefited as a result. Working offspring who made such contributions were often exempted from household chores and enjoyed considerable independence.

It appears that over the history of the colonial-industrial period there have been different reasons for co-residence at different times. But not until now, it seems, has it been a result of the inability of the young to support themselves. It appears that in the late twentieth century, the general social status of the young is lower than it was in the mid-twentieth century, and is perhaps even lower than in the mid-nineteenth century. If these speculations are true, we have witnessed a general slide in the overall status of the young.

The Overall Impact of Institutional Changes

A broad picture emerges from the above institutional analysis of youth in the workplace, as seekers of educational credentials, and as increasingly dependent on "safety net parents," and of the prolongation of youth as a period of life. In comparative terms, young people have gone from (a) beings assets of their parents to being liabilities; (b) being socially valued as workers to being socially assigned as students; and (c) being producers in a society that recognized their contributions to being consumers in a society that gives them insufficient means to satisfy their material appetites.

These trends have combined to introduce several contradictions into the lives of young people and their parents. For example, many parents with adult children living at home are in a sense subsidizing the industries that pay their offspring so little, as well as those that sell their offspring expensive consumer items. According to Palladino (1996), in the United States, teenagers currently constitute "a red-hot consumer market worth $89 billion," not counting the $200 billion their parents spend on them. This is a tenfold increase over the past 40 years.

At the same time, many young people living with their parents can only find minimum-wage jobs that do not allow for independent living. Caught in this situation, young people often spend their meagre earnings on immediate gratification instead of saving for eventual independence. One American study of working secondary school students noted that "when asked about their motivations for employment, they emphasize the monetary rewards," and most of this discretionary income "supports a high level of self-indulgent consumption." This consumption is most often of clothing (among 70% of those studied), and secondarily of items like "records, tapes, sports equipment, stereos, TVs, bikes," and only 7% admitted giving money to their families" (Fine, Mortimer, and Roberts 1990). Though rare, some have also been known to put away some money for future educational endeavours.

This generally frivolous use of their money increases their financial dependence on their parents, delaying even longer their departure from the parental home. As a result, their youth is prolonged further, and full adulthood is postponed even more.

The Emergence of the Ideology of Youth

It is quite curious that more people have not expressed greater concern about how things have worked out for young people in Canadian society. One might have expected more public outcry, marked by frequent demonstrations or some sort of political mobilization. There *has* been disaffection, but there are few signs that there will be any concerted effort to remedy the situation. When a muted response is found to conditions such as those described above, it is often due to ideological manipulations of public perceptions about the nature of the problem.

It appears that if the changing material conditions noted above are acknowledged at all, they are thought of as historical inevitabilities. But the changes that have taken place in the workplace, the education system, and the structure of family were not inevitable. Clearly, the direction of change and who benefited from the changes was influenced by those who had the most say in these things: those in the oldest age groups controlling business and government. Yet, if we were to review media discussions of these issues, we would most likely see the problem framed as a baby boomer–baby buster conflict, with baby boomers portrayed as the "greedy bad guys." As we saw, however, it is the pre-baby boomers who have benefited most from changes over the past 20 years, while baby boomers have actually suffered losses (see Table 5.2). But, even this media-produced distraction from the issues is only part of the story. To get a sense of how public perception about young people might have been manipulated with the net effect of diminishing their status, it is necessary to take a longer historical view.

Part of the diminishing status of young people can be traced to negative stereotypes. Those negative stereotypes gained legitimacy in the late nineteenth century, when the renowned psychologist G. Stanley Hall formulated the "storm and stress" model of adolescence. This marked the "discovery" of "adolescence" as a social problem by social scientists. Before this time, "young people" were not as clearly distinguished from "older people" as they are now, partly because fewer people grew old. Being younger was simply more normal. As we saw in Table 5.1, a century or more ago those between ages 15 and 29 made up about half of the adult population, and the median age was 20 or less. In fact, it was not until the late 1930s that the term "teenager" was even coined.

Hall's work created the widespread belief that adolescence is a period distinct from both childhood and adulthood, characterized by hormonally stimulated turmoil. Hall and others argued that it does not matter what experiences and opportunities are available to the young, for all must pass through this period of storm and stress. But adolescence is a cultural institution, not a biological phenomenon, and the storm-and-stress model has been discounted by recent research. However, the net effect was that the labels stuck, and with them this segment of the population was singled out for special treatment.

We will not dwell on all the implications of the storm-and-stress model except to say that it has prevailed during the twentieth century in several of the social sciences and has indelibly stamped public consciousness. The psychopathology attributed to adolescence came to be used as a justification for the juvenile justice system in North America and the suspension of rights of adolescents imposed by that system. These conditions have been accompanied by widespread discrimination towards the young, not only in the workplace, but in their day-to-day lives, when they are denied access to restaurants, stores, and other public places.

Thus, what has happened over this century is that, in an attempt to understand and protect "young people," social science appears to have prejudiced public consciousness and public policy against them. What has developed is an exaggerated tendency to see the young person as "afflicted" with the "condition" of adolescence, even to the extent that some psychiatrists tend to see adolescence itself as a "disorder" with various sets of symptoms.

These attitudes may have contributed to the marginalization of young people and their exclusion from adult society, affecting how changing material conditions played out in the workplace, the educational system, and the family. As shown above, young people have increasingly been kept in holding patterns before being allowed entry into adulthood and full productive participation in the community. Thus, the twentieth-century "ideology of youth," which views adolescence more as a biological phenomenon than a cultural institution, may have helped justify the disenfranchisement of this age group, particularly teenagers.

Unlike women and racial minorities, it is still considered legitimate to speak of the young adult as somehow biologically unsuitable for full participation in society (Males 1996). However, we believe that it is more than a coincidence that the ideology of youth, which emerged in the twentieth century, nicely complements the fact that, when youth labour is needed at all, it is mainly used in subordinate service positions. It would be much better, and more just, to acknowledge that technological displacement and changing competition ratios are responsible, than to continue to find fault with young adults. So, instead of having this segment of the population competing with older workers for the more valued and rewarding jobs, we find that it is now accepted as "normal" for many people under 25 (and even 30) years of age to have their transition to adulthood and independence delayed because of beliefs about some "defect" when a century or two ago they would have spent more of their lives in productive activities.

Talking Directly to Youth

After the publication of *Generation on Hold* in 1994, the most common question journalists asked us was what solutions we could recommend to young people themselves, and to society as a whole, to remedy age-based inequalities experienced by young people. In that book, we offered some; here we offer several more.

For young people themselves, a number of personal adjustments can be made:

- Be informed about who benefits and who loses as a result of certain economic changes — this is an antidote for self-blame. Combat apathy, and become involved in the political affairs of your community.

- Resist indoctrination pressures that draw people into the mindless consumer role. (This ranges from peer pressure, through advertising strategies, to political propaganda.)

- Work to develop a meaningful philosophy of life not solely predicated on consumerism, materialism, or hedonism; balance the "pleasure principle" and the "reality principle" (i.e., have fun, but realize there are real issues that affect your long-term happiness and well-being).

- Think about what constitutes "success" for you, rather than what other people think. (There are non-status–seeking forms of success, like being good at caring for others, and contributing to the general social betterment of the community.)

- Discover your own "special competency," namely, what you are really good at and feel good doing. (But don't worry if what you are good at is not part of middle-class definitions of success.)

- Take advantage of the prolonged period of youth imposed on you to develop your "real" self instead of the self others want you to be for them (i.e., be true to yourself, and don't try to please others just for its own sake).

- If you are locked out of adult independence, make the best of it in a way that enriches your life; and consider the real possibility that your adulthood will not be based on the middle-class model of the mid-twentieth century. (In fact, you may be ahead of the times because it is a real possibility that everyone will have to adopt sustainable lifestyles for a sustainable planet for ecological reasons.)

At the collective level, we recommend that young people themselves create a youth movement modelled after the "grey power" movement, the environmental movement, or the women's movement. Activities might include the following:

- Political lobbying (e.g., through student federations).

- Pushing for the formation of well-funded youth councils (as in the Scandinavian countries) run by young people to monitor problems, conduct research, and make policy recommendations. (Canada has one such organization as far as we know — the Canadian Youth Foundation.)

- Joining or forming a political party which speaks to youth interests. (This party could mobilize the 18- to 29-year-old vote, which amounts to almost 30% of eligible voters — compare with the Bloc Québécois, which is a single-interest party ostensibly representing 30% of Canadian voters, yet for a time it was the official opposition in Canada's Parliament.)

- Boycotting products, media, and other institutions or organizations that manipulate young people and attempt to turn them into mindless, passive consumers.

At the level of political economy, the state needs to reverse its recent neglect of youth issues and focus on the following:

- Adopt active versus passive employment practices. (The Canadian Youth Foundation [1995] puts the hidden costs of youth inequality at $4.5 billion a year in unemployment benefits and social assistance, e.g., Sweden of the 1980s provides a model for active policies.)

- Build the social capital of communities — the so-called third sector — by providing social wages (e.g., for work with non-profit, volunteer, and community organizations) and shadow wages (i.e., through tax deductions for voluntary work in the community at large).

- Create jobs for young people by encouraging job sharing and shorter work weeks with economic incentives (i.e., state subsidies topping up lower wages, which in turn save on unemployment benefits and social assistance).

- Tax the profits made by transnationals, so money is invested in the communities from which it is taken.

If all of these things were done, we believe many of the problems of young people would be mitigated. Through these efforts, the shape of capitalism can be fundamentally altered and redirected so that it does not run counter to the goals of social justice and does not amount to mere reformism. However, this task requires both individual initiative and political will. It remains to be seen whether Canadians, who are known for their passive acceptance of authority, can rise to the occasion.

Intergenerational Justice

In the foregoing we have been articulating a concern for intergenerational justice, namely, the responsibilities generations have for each other's welfare and the sharing of collective resources. But there is a serious generation gap, not in the simple sense of parents and their children not understanding each other, but in terms of hostilities among different age groups based on perceived self-interest. Indeed, "us–them" antagonisms seem to be growing, and age-based blame and recrimination are now widespread. Thus, we have a new area of intergroup relations emerging where many people — not just teens — are "tribalizing" with their age-mates. This tribalization gives people a sense of "rightness" in terms of their privilege or oppression as against the privilege or oppression of people from other age groups.

Such intergenerational tensions are familiar, and are media favourites. Two particularly high-profile tensions are (a) the elderly who fear and loathe teens, and (b) baby busters who dismiss baby boomers as greedy and self-indulgent. In his 1996 study of intergenerational justice in the United States, *Generations and the Challenge of Justice*, D.E. Lee identified the following tensions:

- "The tendency to find fault with other generations is common to all generations";

- "Many members of all generations falsely assume that their experiences either have been or can be duplicated by members of other generations";

- "Many members of younger generations have high anger levels related to the taxes they pay to finance benefits for older generations";

- "Members of older generations who came of age when good jobs with decent wages were readily available have little understanding of the job anxiety and economic insecurity experienced by many who are younger."

However widespread these tensions are, it is clear that in the interests of justice they must be set aside so we can get down to the business of creating a more equitable society where age is not a basis for discrimination. This may sound idealistic in a society with a recent history of "tribal self-interest," but justice must be based on ideals. Given their economic underpinnings, D.E. Lee believed these generation gaps are more serious than any we have seen in the past. In his view, they are not issues that can be put off, for if they are, there may be dire consequences: "We will be strained to the breaking point if we cannot articulate a shared sense of justice based on inclusiveness and the affirmation of the dignity and significance of those of all ages. We will be torn apart if we are not responsive to the concerns and well-being of young and old alike. The years to come will be disastrous if we plunge headlong into the chasm of a war between the generations."

Thus, we have various age groups fighting with each other over their share of the pie to the point that serious animosities seem to be emerging. Yet, in blaming each other, people miss the real cause of their financial troubles, namely, an economic system in which 20% of the population controls 70% of the wealth. And, as we know, for reasons of social control and political order, it is very useful for that 20% of the population to have the other 80% distracted and fighting over their 30% share of the wealth.

Conclusion

Some critics might read the above and argue that there have been periods when it was tough to be young in many societies. For example, during the Great Depression, poverty and despair were widespread and forced many young people to move about the country looking for work. During the two world wars, thousands of young Canadians lost their lives. Young people have faced war and famine throughout history, and the physical consequences were far greater than what most young people are facing today. Critics might also add that the affluence of Canadian society makes comparisons relative: Is it not much better to be non-affluent in contemporary Canada than in the Canada of 200 years ago, or in a developing country? The answer to this last question is probably yes. But that must not distract us from trying to discover how things got this way, and why things did not work out more equally over this century.

The future certainly holds promise for some; indeed, change can bring great benefits as old interest groups lose their power and conventions change. However, a key issue for the future is whether the inequalities identified here constitute part of a cycle or part of a long-term trend. Unfortunately, a consensus is emerging that workplace changes are part of long-term structural changes. In fact, two long-term trends appear to have set in, one in the workplace and one in the educational system.

If the current trend of technological displacement continues unabated in the workplace, it is likely that we will see a continuing reduction in the size of what people think of as the "middle class" in the next century, along with a continuing polarization of income. This polarization could reshape the class structure of advanced societies, returning to a more blatant two-class system, with little resembling the "middle class" of the twentieth century. Up to 80% of workers will be needed for low-wage jobs, particularly in subordinate service work. Accordingly, only about 20% of workers will be needed to bring their considerable expertise to design and maintain the technology and to manage complex technical systems. More and more young people in each generation will find themselves members of a working class that engulfs 80% of the population in work that is clearly undesirable in terms of wages, benefits, security, and working conditions. There will be large numbers of working poor, and many unemployed, underemployed, and unemployable people. Because the young are often the hardest hit by such changes, we may see a realignment of occupational and class structures based partly on age, with the poorest segment being drawn largely from the youth population. Moreover, once in the poorest segment of this new working class, people will likely remain there throughout their lives. If this happens, most people will face the prospect that they will not do as well financially or occupationally as their parents; the "middle class" lifestyle of the second half of the twentieth century will be a thing of the past.

Economic globalization is currently exacerbating this problem as capital continues to leave Canada in search of cheap labour and lucrative markets elsewhere. This has meant fewer tax revenues from that capital, which could otherwise have been reinvested in the communities from which the profit was extracted. In turn, it has been even more difficult for governments to reduce the deficits produced by the inflation of the past 20 years, leading them to set aside many of the obligations they had assumed in the twentieth century, including assistance to the disadvantaged and support for two mainstays of so-called middle-class employment — health care and education. And so we see a complex set of circumstances that contribute to the downward spiral of the "middle class."

Because of the technical skills it imparts, what remains of the higher educational system after government retrenchment will likely be increasingly important in determining who has access to the relatively small number of lucrative high-tech jobs. But, social class advantage will likely come into play, as parents already positioned in the lucrative sector give special guidance to their children and provide "social capital" for them. Thus, we may see a situation where education is an uncontested means of reproduction of social classes, as it was before governments attempted to correct class-based injustices.

Demographic change may mitigate these long-term trends. We may witness another phase in a cycle where the fortunes of the young improve. This demographic change hinges on the movement of baby boomers out of the labour force. Most of them will retire between 2010 and 2030, with retirements peaking around 2020. As seniors, the baby boomers will constitute a formidable market for goods and services, so the labour force will benefit by providing them. It is possible that this shift will begin earlier, with a significant proportion of baby boomers taking early retirement beginning in 2001 when the first of them reach their mid-fifties.

The down-side of these demographic changes is that most of the jobs produced in this cycle will likely be in low-level service positions. However, there may also be a greater demand for higher level financial, information, and health care services that could offset this trend. Regardless, because of improved health care and the consequent increased human longevity, it is unlikely that the competition ratio will ever favour the young worker again.

Earlier predictions that the smaller baby bust generation would be in greater demand in the labour market were not borne out, mainly because of technological displacement (cf. Morissette, Myles, and Picot 1993; Myles, Picot, and Wannell 1988). As well, when the baby boom generation passes through, the population "pyramid" will more closely resemble a vase than a pyramid, especially if fertility remains low. This is likely to lead to a situation where the few young people will have to support a large number of retirees. Indeed, by 2036 the median population age will be somewhere between 41 and 50 depending on fertility patterns (McKie 1993).

What lies beyond these demographic trends is difficult to say. Just how much more technological displacement will take place, and how much educational credentials will continue to inflate, is also difficult to say. Certainly, there will be peaks and plateaus to these trends. For example, we may have reached a plateau in the chase after credentials, with the recent levelling in university attendance. But, the danger with trends like technological displacement is that one company's employee is another company's consumer: when a company lays off one of its employees, it is also laying off a purchaser of goods and services. In spite of the ability of capitalism to survive such crises in the past, it is only a matter of time before companies collapse because of overproduction; if this becomes widespread, the entire economy can collapse. If that happens, the cleavages and fractures that underlie Canadian society may well come to the surface and conflict among different age groups could become more overt. Certainly, if a majority of young people continue to find themselves locked into lifelong poverty, this conflict could lead to violence motivated by vengeance and a desire for social justice. Recognizing the class basis for intergenerational inequalities is the first step to bringing about a more just society.

6

The Faces of Inequality Under Capitalism

In George Orwell's classic work of fiction, *Nineteen Eighty-Four*, he painted a picture of alienation, oppression, and hopelessness among the citizens of "Oceania" that many in the West associated with the hapless people of the Soviet Union, and that many today might associate with the youth of Canada and elsewhere. Because of the pervasive and effective system of social control in Oceania, and because the better educated, middle-class citizens were so brainwashed by the ideology of "Big Brother" (the inner circle of political leaders), there was little likelihood that an opposition would develop, or that meaningful change would ever come from the "Party" or from the better-off segments of society. But unwilling to accept the dismal fate dictated by the Party, Winston, the protagonist in the book, felt that the only salvation for Oceania lay with the exploited and oppressed workers: the proletarian masses or so-called proles. Thus, he wrote in his diary, "If there is hope it lies in the proles." Indeed, Orwell goes on to emphasize that hope *"must* lie in the proles."

By extension, given the pervasiveness of the dominant ideologies of liberalism, individualism, consumerism, and materialism in contemporary Canadian society, if there is to be hope for the future, we might just paraphrase Orwell and say that it *must* lie with the young. They are the ones who *must* find a way to transcend the ideology of corporate capitalism. Not only does the future belong to youth in the clichéd sense, but it is among them that we can see a narrowing of the divisions along race and gender lines we have been discussing. Those divisions that have marked the country's history to date, and have generally distracted Canadians from developing a class awareness of their society, are increasingly coming to be seen as socially conditioned, and not as naturally ordained.

Broadly speaking, as inter-ethnic marriages or sexual liaisons become more common, as children of those unions increase in number and visibility throughout society, as gender differences that separated previous generations become eroded by legislation and modern social consciousness, as capital and consumer markets continue to homogenize the population through such phenomena as deskilling and mass advertising, the terms of social and political engagement will vastly change. Hence, the *hope* in the long run (and we stress the word "hope") is that young women and men who share similar lifestyles, who have roughly equivalent levels of education, income, and cultural capital, and who are growing progressively impatient with the ideologies of racism and sexism will emerge as the best placed to address the problems of continuing social inequality in Canada. Their challenge will be to overcome the persistence of ageism, while directing their combined energies to the fundamental class divisions of capitalism that are likely to survive race, gender, and youth inequality. We must emphasize, however, that the accumulation of race, gender, age, and class inequalities does not have a mere *additive* effect. Rather, as the black feminist writer Patricia Hill-Collins notes, the effect is better understood as *multiplicative*, since no type of simple reductionism can ever hope to capture the qualitative nature of the oppressions involved. So, how does one manufacture consensus or combine energies among young people when ethnic, gender, and class entrepreneurs are so keen on dividing them? Is this mere unbridled idealism?

The Vertical Mosaic

Canadian society was characterized by John Porter in 1965 as a mosaic — a vertical mosaic in which various ethnic groups have fit together in a class-based hierarchy of wealth, privilege, and power. More recently, Queen's University sociologist Roberta Hamilton has called it a "gendered vertical mosaic," in which men (husbands and fathers) enjoy myriad social privileges at the expense of women. However one wishes to characterize Canadian society metaphorically, it is clear from what we have discussed that in recent years its class structure has changed in some respects. Changes have resulted from immigration, demographics, technological displacement, affirmative action, globalization, and other forces.

Some of these changes have brought about an ethnic diversification of the Canadian bourgeoisie, which is no longer dominated by Anglos. In fact, the global face of capital is certainly not distinguished by race, and this is having an increasing impact in Canada, as the forces of globalization reshape its economy. As for the working class, its face is not strictly defined by race, sex, or age, except as these designations are conducive to targeting various groups as sources of cheap labour. Because capital has no race, sex, religion, or national allegiance, we have also seen how, as the conditions for capital accumulation change, different groups are targeted for exploitation: indigenous peoples, blacks, women, poor whites, and so on. To this list we might add the recent focus on the young, who are being rapidly disenfranchised socially, occupationally, and economically.

In Chapter 1 we argued that inequality is a defining feature of capitalism. Because the economic structure of society is premised upon a fundamental inequality in the ownership of productive property, one cannot meaningfully speak of capitalism and equality synonymously. The non-owners of property must work for wages in order to survive, and in the process they create vast wealth for those who employ them. In Chapter 2 we showed how, over the years, the increasing proportion of non-owners (the proletarianization of former independent producers) has been accompanied by a shrinking number of owners (the concentration of capital in fewer hands). Canada's maturity as a leading industrial capitalist country has thus mirrored changes that have taken place in other similarly placed countries, particularly as these changes relate to wider patterns of inequality in the society.

The ethno-racial composition of the Canadian class structure, for example, is shifting as some non-Anglos, especially those of Japanese, Korean, and Chinese descent, improve their positions (Forcese 1996:87-90). These changes are also echoed in the make-up of the Canadian middle class, which was at one time overwhelmingly British and French in origin, but now includes many Jews and people of German, Dutch, and Ukrainian descent (Driedger 1996:198-199; 246-248). Further, women are making gains at home, at school, and in the workplace, especially younger women, while men's past advantages are declining. But just as matters appear generally to be improving for the next generation of Canadians, we have noted a contradictory reversal along the age dimension. Whereas throughout Canadian history every generation was able to do better than the previous one, this is no longer the case. Older Canadians have benefited from shifts in wealth over this century — more secure jobs and pensions, better health care, and cheaper housing. This contrasts with the fortunes of younger Canadians, particularly young men, who have lost out as a result of those economic crises occasioned by the excesses of older generations.

Among social commentators, nevertheless, there is still a great deal of controversy regarding some of the above-mentioned changes. Turning to race and gender, for instance, there are those who see positive changes in the positions of these previously disadvantaged groups. However, those changes are seen by some as minimal for we still hear complaints from these very sectors of persisting racial and gender discrimination associated with educational and employment equity practices. It appears that the Canadian workplace is the scene of conflict as individuals and groups struggle for some advantage in the competitive capitalist economy. Just what do we make of such contradictory claims? And, how are they likely to be resolved?

Beyond Identity Politics: The Importance of Class

The current situation in Canada can be understood in terms of the divide-and-conquer strategy that creates and maintains intergroup hostilities as a means of diverting attention away from the real sources of inequalities. The more individual men and women, black and white, young and old, compete with each other over jobs and wages, the less attention the capitalists and corporate elites receive. Thus, in Chapter 4 we documented how this competition has led to a decline in the earning power and employability of men as a group, not to an overall improvement in the lives of Canadians, and we went on to charge that young women's recent near-parity with men is due more to this decline than to a rise in the fortunes of young women. Similarly, the more individuals from various ethnic groups compete with, and perhaps resent, one another, the more the real sources of their social and economic disadvantage escape scrutiny.

One way to illustrate this is to examine figures that correlate the population with the ownership of wealth in Canada (see Table 2.4, Chapter 2). There are various estimates of how this wealth is divided among Canadians, but a clear pattern of income and wealth concentration is evident. In *Controlling Interest: Who Controls Canada?*, Diane Francis noted that just twelve families and five conglomerates control one-third of all corporate assets in the country. Statistics Canada reported that the income of the top quintile of the population is over nine times the amount of the bottom quintile (Cat. No. 13-207 1992:147). University of Western Ontario economist James Davies shows that the top 20% of the population owns or controls about 70% of the wealth (1993:108). What this means is that the other 80% of

Canadians must share the remaining 30% of the wealth. Little wonder, then, that there is so much competition, strife, and resentment, especially among those who aspire to the affluence and lifestyles of the new middle class. Instead of fighting among one another, a simplistic argument would hold that the 80% segment of the population needs to develop a political consciousness and direct its attention to the practices and lifestyles of the wealthy and comfortable 20% segment. We are referring here to the inordinate attention that segment receives from governments in the form of tax breaks, bailouts, government-sponsored investment insurance, and trade protection legislation. If it were possible for the neglected 80% to unite their vote, the simplistic argument continues, they could conceivably form their own political party and easily elect a federal government to see to their interests.

Unfortunately, this is unlikely to happen. Why? Because that 80% of the population does not form a homogeneous whole with common economic and political interests. They continue to be divided along lines of race, gender, regional identity, and so on. The manufacture of consent has been so successful over this century that a large percentage of the voting public has been convinced that corporate interests are also their own interests. This manufacture of consent dates back to the 1920s, when universal suffrage was put in place and when those in power realized that they needed to influence voters by shaping public opinion to suit corporate interests. They worked at this for decades, and by all accounts they have succeeded. This is how we can explain the general lack of political will to oppose the corporate agenda and the amoral practices that daily violate both the human community and the environment, and the simultaneous acceptance of the neo-conservative agenda of deficit fighting.

The distribution of wealth in Canada cannot be divorced from the fact that international capital has been siphoning wealth out of the country, a process made even easier by the North American Free Trade Agreement and sustained by the type of thinking that accepts the "inevitability" of globalization. The distribution of wealth has also been affected by the technological displacement that has fundamentally altered many workplaces and job structures, and affected families of all social classes. From the perspective of retail sales, for example, every laid-off worker is potentially a laid-off consumer, and when that worker is the main breadwinner of a family, the effect is multiplied.

Following the discussion in Chapter 5, it appears that the job picture in Canada is becoming increasingly polarized between a tiny segment of highly skilled and highly paid technical experts, and a large variety of workers in routine or mechanical jobs in the service and related industries. We may in fact be heading towards the situation where only 20% of jobs provide a remuneration currently associated with middle-class affluence, while the remaining 80% will tend to be low-skill, low-pay, terminal or contract positions. Thus, a rather disturbing scenario is likely to unfold: a continuing proletarianization and impoverishment of the majority of Canadians based on age. That is, each successive future group of Canadians is likely to be poorer than the last. This may continue until we reach the type of highly volatile situation that makes for social and political instability.

Blending the Generations in the Late Twentieth Century

The impoverishment of youth has affected not just the youngest age groups — those in their teens and twenties — but every age group born since the Second World War. In fact, there is much misunderstanding and confusion about what has happened to each age group over this time period. Just as race and gender rivalries have bedevilled the society, so too age groups dispute who has benefited and who has suffered most from developments since the war. The irony is that these misunderstandings and conflicts, like those related to race and gender, have also directed attention away from the sources of the difficulties that these younger generations have experienced. Accordingly, by way of concluding the book, it is worth devoting some space to this issue, especially since we are convinced that it is to youth we must look if the new millennium is to hold any promise of seriously addressing the problem of Canada's social inequalities.

Much has been said and written in the media about the various age groups born since the Second World War: so-called baby boomers have been accused of being greedy and self-absorbed, and so-called generation Xers have been called whiners and slackers. Such characterizations often amount to little more than stereotypes, negative labelling, and overgeneralizations. They also tend to personalize age groups, as if it is somehow people's "fault" that they were born in a certain year that coincides with one of the labels. Thus, we find another example of victim blaming, where the larger picture is ignored in favour of individualistic, psychological explanations.

Table 6.1

The Post–Second World War Cohorts

	I	II	III	IV
Year Born:	1945–54	1955–64	1965–74	1975–84
Labels:	Early Boomers	Late Boomers	Busters	McBoomers
Ages in 1997:	43–52	33–42	23–32	13–22
Parents' Birth Cohort:	1915–24	1925–34	1935–44	1945–54

Source: Allahar and Côté.

As sociologists, we are not interested in stereotypes associated with personality characteristics, as if the year one was born can predict how lazy or greedy one is. We prefer to leave that sort of stuff to astrologers. Instead, we deal with these issues at the aggregate level, using concepts that help us understand long-term and widespread societal trends. Hence, we adopt here a "cohort analysis" to help us examine what age-groups have in common and how they differ at the aggregate level. For our purposes, a cohort is any group of people born within a given period of time.

Although useful, we should add some qualifications about the applicability of cohort analysis and its limitations. First, in a cohort analysis not all individuals will be described by a pattern; rather, the experiences of the average member will be taken as the marker for the entire cohort. Assuming that the experiences examined have a "normal distribution" around this average, we can have some confidence that the majority of people in a cohort will be "properly" characterized. Second, this type of analysis is further limited because of the arbitrary dividing lines defining cohorts. Often these lines are based on a combination of significant events or the beginning or midpoint of a decade. Third, individuals born close to the dividing lines may share the experiences of both cohorts, so exceptions may need to be made for them. And fourth, even when differences are identified at the aggregate level, they are differences of degree, not kind. In the cohorts we examine, certain commonalities are reflected in shared significant experiences (like underemployment), but they differ by degree. Too often cohorts are set apart from each other by the media and general public as if they are different species bent on annihilating one another. Such characterizations simply fuel misdirected intercohort tensions.

Table 6.1 provides a categorization of the post–Second World War cohorts. We have taken the liberty of using easily recognized labels. We can see that a cycle has been completed in generational terms. That is, the first cohort has reproduced itself with the fourth — the early boomers are the parents of the McBoomers. Moreover, the early boomers are increasingly the guardians of the society the McBoomers are entering, and will enter, for another half decade. Hence, as both parents and teachers, the early boomers have reason to be concerned about the plight of the McBoomers. We take this as a good sign from the point of view of intergenerational understanding.

The post–Second World War cohorts have shared certain significant coming-of-age experiences. Viewed from the perspective of their day-to-day lives, these experiences include a convergence of gender roles (the experience of "being" male or "being" female is becoming more similar as more roles are shared); liberal gender relations (males and females as peers and casual lovers versus earlier forms of segregation and sexual puritanism); greater permissiveness accorded them by their parents and society (especially regarding sexual behaviour, drug use, and the use of leisure time); the rise of mass culture and the truly mass media (especially rock music and the television industries); mass segregation in age-graded schools; and expanded opportunities for higher education.

These intercohort experiences have varied by social class and racial or ethnic group. We submit, however, that there are enough similarities to warrant the proposition that the forces shaping cohorts are also affecting the structure of inequality in Canada, thereby creating greater similarities within each successive cohort, regardless of race, class, or gender. While the process is by no means complete, it can be seen in second-generation immigrant families whose cultures differ markedly from Canada's dominant norm. Take, for example, teenaged children who appear to have more in common with their fellow Canadian-born peers than with their parents, and who demand the same freedoms as those peers, like staying out late in mixed-sex groups, drinking alcohol, choosing their own dates, and so on. This process seems to result mainly from the tremendous capacity of capital to use technologies to reach and influence the masses. These technologies have been improved at an astounding pace, permitting the forces of capitalism to be strengthened, most recently on a global basis. Consequently, we live in a "mass-capitalist" society, a world in which increasingly advanced technologies intrude on virtually all aspects of people's day-to-day lives and affect almost every aspect of consumption and production.

Cohort analyses can be employed to illustrate these homogenizing influences in a number of domains. For example, as noted in Chapter 5, the term "teenager" was first coined in the 1930s, but because of the Second World War, the first cohorts to be widely known as "teenagers" by advertisers and merchandisers were the postwar cohorts. We traced the effects of this, noting the paradoxical rise of youth consumerism in spite of a loss of productive earning power. The consequences of this include a prolonged period of youth and dependence on parents.

The homogenizing influences to which we refer can be illustrated by the higher education and work experiences of each cohort as follows.

EARLY BOOMERS

A significant segment of this cohort entered university between 1963 and 1972, during the first enrolment expansion. They were the first to face the prospect of a mass prolongation of youth as "student," although most went only as far as completing high school. They rode the crest of the wave of expanding middle-class opportunities. (But note that these opportunities were enjoyed more so by the cohort before them, those born between 1935 and 1944.) There were good economic opportunities for university graduates, yet many have experienced a decline in earning power since the early 1980s. Although some became well positioned in the expanded middle class, as this has shrunk large numbers have either been squeezed out or live with job insecurity, heavy debt loads, and would face great difficulty in retraining.

LATE BOOMERS

Members of this cohort enrolled in universities in increasing numbers between 1973 and 1982, but they saw the beginning of the underemployment trend. They made the transition to the workplace as the once-expanding middle class began to contract, and there was growing concern that economic opportunities were diminished for some graduates. Thus, underemployment has been a persistant problem, and significant numbers must now accustom themselves to regular job or career changes as institutional downsizing has truncated many careers. For members of this cohort, available work is increasingly contract and unskilled, or is in competition with younger cohorts, and the accompanying economic shortfalls and insecurities make it difficult for many to buy a home or save for retirement.

BUSTERS

They entered university during the 1984–1993 period and were part of the second enrolment expansion, as a majority went on to higher education. They increasingly found themselves caught up in a scramble for increasingly devalued credentials, with growing numbers pursuing postgraduate degrees to gain some relative advantage. They (and others) felt a mounting disillusionment with higher education and, owing to declining job opportunities, some have experienced an increased prolongation of youth as "adults on hold," finding themselves still living with their parents in their late twenties. Many encountered increased competition for jobs with older cohorts and, having amassed student loans in the range of $20 to $30 thousand, felt a growing pessimism regarding even short-term economic opportunities.

MCBOOMERS

They began enroling in universities in 1993 (and will continue to do so until the year 2003). They are among the largest cohort that has gone directly from high school to postsecondary institutions and, as such, are the inheritors of the paradox of inflated credentials (Chapter 5), even while their educational funding is under financial attack by various levels of government. The bulk of this cohort find themselves locked into youth, out of "adulthood," and still living with their parents. The "perfunctory student" becomes a model for many — any degree will do. They witness the collapse of middle-class opportunities for their parents and the other two cohorts as governments retreat to fight deficits and corporations downsize in spite of record profits. The "good" jobs that might have been theirs are taken by older cohorts who are themselves under pressure, and because only "McJobs" are available for most, the short- and long-term economic prospects appear dismal for many.

Thus, we have four cohorts with varying degrees of shared educational and work experiences that have reason to find common cause for complaint independent of race and gender issues, although these are still very real for many and complicate the matter in no small way. Certainly, the 1980s and 1990s have been hard on members of all four cohorts, but to varying degrees. Yet we find certain tensions and resentments among them, especially between the two boomer cohorts, on the one hand, and the two later ones, on the other.

The questions are, then, how can members of these cohorts develop the political awareness that is necessary if they are to arrive at a structural understanding of their situation? Do they, in fact, have a common predicament that can override their potential age, ethnic, and gender differences and unite them on a class basis?

Conclusion: Learning to Love Corporate Capitalism?

Just as some may dismiss as a "fact of life" the predicament in which many young people find themselves, others may dismiss as a "fact of life" the conditions of capitalism that have created the other inequalities we have identified. These critics might argue that capitalism is here to stay, and in spite of its faults, is the best available system, given the human propensity to self-interest and greed. They might also defend this position by arguing that those people, young or otherwise, with the most talent, and who work the hardest, will in the end realize their dreams. Young people, however, will have to wait longer than their parents and will have to settle for less.

The implicit ideological message here is that capitalism is the only game in town, and the sooner one learns to play it, the better off he or she will be. The media and other "guardians" of the social order are always keen to remind us how the baby boomers who experimented with alternatives to materialism and consumerism in the 1960s saw the light by the 1970s and gave up their experiments as unworkable. Indeed, many from that cohort who shunned materialism for spiritualism and communalism came back to materialism and individualism, and some have even become very materially successful. Capitalism is a social system that encourages one to be "selfish": to explore one's self indefinitely, to be concerned or even obsessed with feeding one's self-esteem, to feel a right to seek one's self-actualization, and to continually gratify one's sensual self. And, for many, it is not difficult to learn to love such a system that permits one to be so self-indulgent.

As we have argued throughout this book, however, the success stories and the material comforts are largely illusory and spread unevenly among all segments and classes in society. Further, there is no guarantee that capitalism will continue to provide such narcissistic benefits indefinitely. It is becoming increasingly clear that the planet can no longer sustain current levels of consumption and the accompanying waste. But when these are no longer possible, it is certain that capital will move on to other profitable investments. In so doing, it will search out other groups to exploit, and thereby perpetuate, exacerbate, or create new inequalities in Canadian society. This is how one might understand the willing embrace of NAFTA by the political elite — an embrace which exploits cheap Mexican labour while exporting Canadian jobs abroad. This is part of the essential nature of capitalism. Hence, inequalities will remain part of Canada's social landscape as long as the economic logic of capitalism continues to be coupled with the political ideologies of liberalism and individualism, and as long as these dictate the policies of the various levels of government and structure the productive labour activities, consumption patterns, and political options of Canadians.

But, even beyond this, there is a clear challenge to both the economic and political leaders, on the one hand, and the Canadian people, on the other. We noted in Chapter 2 that, five times in the past six years, Canada has been named by the United Nations as the best country in the world in which to live. This is because of the very high average standard of living of the population and the overall quality of life of its citizens. These in turn are related to the fact that Canada's economy is strong and competitive: its products are in demand both locally and around the world, for while of equivalent quality, Canadian goods and services are better priced than those of other countries.

Competitive pricing, however, is related to competitive labour costs. Those who are able to pay lower prices for labour and still produce a product of high quality will capture the market and triumph over competitors. And as we know, racial and gender inequalities that ensure, for example, that blacks and women can be paid less than others, serve directly to cheapen the price of labour. Thus, the social inequalities we have analyzed in this book are not merely incidental to capitalism, but are rather structurally and intimately tied to Canada's high standard of living. And herein lies the challenge: will Canadians be prepared to work for the elimination of social inequality based on race, gender, age, and class if it will cost them their number one world ranking?

References

Acosta-Belén, E., and C.E. Bose. (1990) "From Structural Subordination to Empowerment: Women and Development in Third World Contexts." *Gender and Society*, vol. 4, no. 3, pp. 299–320.

Akyeampong, E.B. (1992) "Discouraged Workers — Where Have They Gone?" *Perspectives on Labour and Income*, vol. 4, no. 3 (Autumn) pp. 38–44.

Allahar, A.L. (1995a) *Sociology and the Periphery: Theories and Issues*, 2nd ed. Toronto: Garamond.

Allahar, A.L. (1995b) "Women, Feminism and Socialism in Cuba." *Inter-American Review of Bibliography*, vol. 45, nos. 1–2, pp. 53–72.

Allahar, A.L. (1994a) "More than an Oxymoron: The Social Construction of Primordial Attachment" *Canadian Ethnic Studies*, vol. 26, no. 3, pp. 18–33.

Allahar, A.L. (1994b) "Women and the Family in Cuba: A Study Across Time" *Humboldt Journal of Social Relations*, vol. 20, no. 1, pp. 87–120.

Allahar, A.L. (1993) "When Black First Became Worth Less." *International Journal of Comparative Sociology*, vol. 34, nos. 1–2, pp. 39–55.

Allahar, A.L. (1991) "Manufacturing Legitimacy: Ideology, Politics, and Canada's Third World Foreign Policy" in Jamie Swift and Brian Tomlinson (eds.), *Conflicts of Interest: Canada and the Third World*. Toronto: Between-the-Lines, pp. 295–318.

Allahar, A.L. (1987) "Ideology, Social Order, and Social Change," in R. Jack Richardson and Lorne Tepperman (eds.), *The Social World*. Toronto: McGraw-Hill Ryerson, pp. 355–80.

Anderson, D. (1991) *The Unfinished Revolution: The Status of Women in Twelve Countries*. Toronto: Doubleday.

Anderson, K. (1991) *Chain Her by One Foot: The Subjugation of Women in Seventeenth Century New France*. London: Routledge.

Armstrong, P., and H. Armstrong. (1994) *The Double Ghetto: Canadian Women and Their Segregated Work*. Toronto: McClelland and Stewart.

Association of Universities and Colleges in Canada (AUCC). (1996) *Trends 1996: The Canadian University in Profile*. Ottawa: Author.

Baldus, B. (1977) "Social Control in Capitalist Societies: An Examination of the Problem of Order in Liberal Democracies." *Canadian Journal of Sociology*, vol. 2, pp. 37–52.

Bem, S.L., and D.J. Bem. (1970) "Case Study of a Nonconscious Ideology: Training the woman to know her place," in D.J. Bem (ed.). *Beliefs, Attitudes, and Human Affairs*. Belmont, CA: Brooks/Cole, pp. 89–99.

Ben-Tovim, G., J. Gabriel, I. Law, and K. Stredder. (1986) "A Political Analysis of Local Struggles for Racial Equality," in John Rex and David Mason (eds.), *Theories of Race and Ethnic Relations*. Cambridge: Cambridge University Press, pp. 131–52.

Bernard, J. (1981) "The Good-Provider Role: Its Rise and Fall." *American Psychologist*, vol. 36, pp. 1–12.

Best, P. (1995) "Women, Men and Work" *Canadian Social Trends*, no. 36, (Spring), Ottawa: Statistics Canada, pp. 30–3.

Betcherman, G. and R. Morissette. (1994) *Recent Youth Labour Market Experiences in Canada (Analytic studies branch research paper series no. 63)*. Ottawa: Statistics Canada.

Béteille, A. (ed). (1969) *Social Inequality: Selected Readings*. Middlesex, England: Penguin.

Bethke Elshtain, J. (1993) *Democracy on Trial*. Toronto: Anansi.

Bibby, R.W. (1993) *Unknown Gods: The Ongoing Story of Religion in Canada*. Toronto: Stoddart.

Bibby, R.W., and D. C. Posterski. (1992) *Teen Trends: A Nation in Motion*. Toronto: Stoddart.

Bissoondath, N. (1994) *Selling Illusions: The Cult of Multiculturalism in Canada*. Toronto: Penguin.

Bottomore, T. (1979) *Political Sociology*. New York: Harper and Row.

Bourrie, M. (1995) "How Canada's Rich Stay Rich." *The London Free Press*, 21 Oct., p. E1.

Boyd, M., and D. Norris. (1995) "Leaving the Nest? The Impact of Family Structure" in *Canadian Social Trends*, no. 38. (Autumn), Ottawa: Statistics Canada, pp. 14–17.

Bureau of Agriculture and Statistics, Census Dept. (1863) *Census of the Canadas. 1860–61 Personal census*, vol. 1. Mountain Hill, Quebec: S.B. Foote.

Campaign 2000. (1993) *Countdown 93: Child Poverty Indicator Report*. Ottawa: Canadian Council on Social Development.

Canadian Ethnic Studies Association Bulletin. (1992) Vol. 19, no. 2.

Canadian Social Trends. (1994) "Working Teens." No. 35 (Winter), Ottawa: Statistics Canada, pp. 18–22.

Canadian Social Trends. (1995) "Life Expectancy." No. 39 (Winter), Ottawa: Statistics Canada, p. 36.

Canadian Youth Foundation. (1995) *Youth Unemployment: Canada's Hidden Deficit*. Ottawa: Author.

Census Office. (1906) *Fourth Census of Canada 1901, vol. 4, Vital statistics*. Ottawa: S.E. Dawson.

Chomsky, N. (1987) *On Power and Ideology*. Montreal: Black Rose Books.

Chui, T. (1996) "Canada's Population: Charting into the 21st Century," in *Canadian Social Trends*, no. 42 (Autumn), Ottawa: Statistics Canada, pp. 3–7.

Clement, W. (1993) "Property, Labour and Class Relations," in J. Curtis, E. Grabb and N. Guppy (eds.), *Social Inequality in Canada: Patterns, Problems, Policies*, 2nd ed. Toronto: Prentice-Hall, pp. 4–11.

Clement, W. (1975) *The Canadian Corporate Elite: An Analysis of Economic Power.* Toronto: McClelland and Stewart.

Coish, D., and A. Hale. (1994) "The Wage Gap Betwen Men and Women: An Update," in *Dynamics of Labour and Income*. Ottawa: Statistics Canada, pp. 35–41.

Collins, R. (1979) *The Credential Society: A Historical Sociology of Education and Stratification.* New York: Academic Press.

Corbett, D.C. (1957) *Canada's Immigration Policy: A Critique.* Toronto: University of Toronto Press.

Côté, J.E. (1994) *Adolescent Storm and Stress: An Evaluation of the Mead/Freeman Controversy.* Hillsdale, NJ: Lawrence Erlbaum.

Côté, J.E., and A.L. Allahar. (1994) *Generation on Hold: Coming of Age in the Late Twentieth Century.* Toronto: Stoddart.

Coupland, D. (1991) *Generation X: Tales for an Accelerated Culture.* New York: St. Martin's Press.

Crompton, S. (1996) "Employment Prospects for High School Graduates." *Education Quarterly Review*, vol. 3, pp. 8–19.

Crompton, S., and L. Geran. (1995) "Women as Main Wage-earners." in *Perspectives on Labour and Income*, vol. 7, no. 4 (Winter), pp. 26–29.

Cuñeo, C.J. (1996). "International Images of Social Inequality: A Ten-Country Comparison," in A. Frizzell and J.H. Pammett (eds.), *Social Inequality in Canada*. Ottawa: Carleton University Press, pp. 31–66.

D'Emilio, F. (1996) "Mamma Mia! Gen X Clings to Home in Italy." *Ottawa Citizen*, 20 April, p. B1.

D'Souza, D. (1991) *Illiberal Education: the Politics of Race and Sex on Campus.* New York: Free Press.

Dahrendorf, R. (1968) "On the Origin of Inequality among Men," in André Béteille (ed.), *Social Inequality: Selected Readings*. Middlesex, England: Penguin, pp. 16–44.

Dajani, S. (1995) *Eyes Without Country: Searching for a Palestinian Strategy of Liberation.* Philadelphia: Temple University Press.

Danesi, M. (1994) *The Signs and Meanings of Adolescence.* Toronto: University of Toronto Press.

Davetian, B. (1994) "Out of the Melting Pot and Into the Fire." *Canadian Ethnic Studies*, vol. 26, no. 3, pp. 135–40.

Davies, J. (1993) "The Distribution of Wealth and Economic Inequality," in J. Curtis, E. Grabb and N. Guppy (eds.), *Social Inequality in Canada: Patterns, Problems, Policies*, 2nd ed. Toronto: Prentice-Hall, pp. 105–120.

Davies, S., C. Mosher, and B. O'Grady. (1994) "Trends in Labour Market Outcomes of Canadian Post-Secondary Graduates, 1978-1988," in L. Erwin and D. MacLennan (eds.), *Sociology of Education in Canada*. Toronto: Copp Clark Longman, pp. 352–369.

Davis, K., and W.E. Moore. (1970) "Some Principles of Stratification," in Melvin Tumin (ed.), *Readings on Social Stratification*. Englewood Cliffs, NJ: Prentice-Hall, pp. 368–77.

Denis, W.B. (1990) "The Politics of Language," in Peter Li (ed.), *Race and Ethnic Relations in Canada*. Toronto: Oxford University Press, pp. 148–85.

Denton, F.T. (1970) *The Growth of Manpower in Canada*. Ottawa: Dominion Bureau of Statistics.

Department of Agriculture, (1884) *Census of Canada 1880–81*, vol. 2. Ottawa: MacLean, Kager, & Co.

Department of Trade and Commerce. (1925) *Sixth Census of Canada, 1921, vol. 2, Population*. Ottawa: F.A. Acland.

Dominion Bureau of Statistics, (1962) *Specified Age Groups and Sex* (Bulletin SP-1). Ottawa: Minister of Trade and Commerce.

Dominion Bureau of Statistics. (1946) *Eighth Census of Canada 1941: Cross-classifications*. Ottawa: Minister of Trade and Commerce.

Driedger, L. (1996) *Multi-Ethnic Canada: Identities and Inequalities*. Toronto: Oxford University Press.

Driedger, L. (1989) *The Ethnic Factor: Identity in Diversity*. Toronto: McGraw-Hill Ryerson.

Easterlin, R.A. (1978) "What Will 1984 Be like? Socioeconomic Implications of Recent Twists in Age Structure." *Demography*, vol. 15, pp. 397–432.

Economist. (1994) "Generation X-onomics." *Economist*, 19, March, pp. 27–8.

Edgell, S. (1993) *Class*. New York: Routledge.

Elliott, J.L., and A. Fleras. (1992) *Unequal Relations: An Introduction to Race and Ethnic Dynamics in Canada*. Toronto: Prentice-Hall.

Elliott, J.L., and A. Fleras. (1990) "Immigration and the Canadian Ethnic Mosaic," in P.S. Li (ed.), *Race and Ethnic Relations in Canada*. Toronto: Oxford University Press, pp. 51–76.

Ewen, S. (1976) *Captains of Consciousness: Advertising and the Social Roots of the Consumer Culture*. New York: McGraw-Hill.

Fanon, F. (1963) *The Wretched of the Earth*. New York: Grove Press.

Fine, G.A., J.T. Mortimer, and D.F. Roberts. (1990) "Leisure, Work, and the Mass Media," in S.S. Feldman and G.R. Elliott (eds.), *At the Threshold: The Developing Adolescent*. Cambridge, MA: Harvard University Press, pp. 225–52.

Foot, D.K. (1996) *Boom, Bust and Echo: How to Profit from the Coming Demographic Shift.* Toronto: Macfarlane Walter and Ross.

Forcese, D. (1997) *The Canadian Class Structure,* 4th ed. Toronto: McGraw-Hill Ryerson.

Fournier, E., G. Butlin, and P. Giles. (1994) "Intergenerational Change in the Education of Canadians," in *Dynamics of Labour and Income.* Ottawa: Statistics Canada, pp. 24–30.

Francis, D. (1986) *Controlling Interest: Who Owns Canada?* Toronto: Macmillan.

Francis, D. (1984) "Where Will it All End"? *Toronto Star,* 11 Nov., p. 8.

Frideres, J.S. (1988) "Institutional Structures of Economic Deprivation: Native People in Canada," in B. Singh Bolaria and P.S. Li (eds.), *Racial Oppression in Canada,* 2nd ed. Toronto: Garamond, pp. 71–100.

Frideres, J.S. (1976) "Racism in Canada: Alive and Well." *Western Canadian Journal of Anthropology,* vol. 6, pp. 124–46.

Friedman, J.B. (1981) *The Monstrous Races in Medieval Art and Thought.* Cambridge: Harvard University Press.

Frizzell, A., and J.H. Pammett (eds.) (1996) *Social Inequality in Canada.* Ottawa: Carleton University Press.

Galbraith, J.K. (1958) *The Affluent Society.* Boston: Houghton Mifflin.

Galeano, E. (no date) "The Non-Communication Media" in *Nuestra America* (journal). (Translated by Michael Pearlman).

Gaskell, J., A. McLaren, and M. Novogrodsky. (1989) *Claiming an Education: Feminism and Canadian Schools.* Toronto: Our Schools/Our Selves Education Foundation.

Geigen-Miller, P. (1994) "Education No Guarantee Any More." *London Free Press,* 30 April, p. A8.

Giddens, A. (1991) *Modernity and Self-Identity: Self and Society in the Late Modern Age.* Stanford, CA: Standford University Press.

Gilroy, P. (1987) *There Ain't No Black in the Union Jack: The Cultural Politics of Race and Nation.* London: Hutchinson.

Gitlin, T. (1995) *The Twilight of Common Dreams: Why America Is Wracked by Culture Wars.* New York: Henry Holt.

Goode, W. (1980) "Why Men Resist." *Dissent,* vol. 27, pp. 181–93.

Gordon, M. (1964) *Assimilation in American Life: The Role of Race, Religion and National Origins.* New York: Oxford University Press.

Grabb, E.G. (1997) *Theories of Social Inequality: Classical and Contemporary Perspectives,* 3rd ed. Toronto: Harcourt Brace.

Gray, J. (1992) *Men Are from Mars, Women Are from Venus.* New York: HarperCollins.

Gray, J. (1983) "Classical Liberalism, Positional Goods, and the Politicization of Poverty," in A. Ellis and K. Kumar (eds.), *Dilemmas of Liberal Democracies*. London: Tavistock, pp. 174–84.

Gregor, A.D., and G. Jamsin. (1992) *Higher Education in Canada*. Ottawa: Minister of Supply and Service.

Griffiths, N.E.S. (1976) *Penelope's Web*. Toronto: Oxford University Press.

Hamilton, R. (1996) *Gendering the Vertical Mosaic: Feminist Perspectives on Canadian Society*. Toronto: Copp Clark.

Hareven, T.K. (1994) "Aging and Generational Relations: A Historical and Life Course Perspective." *Annual Review of Sociology*, vol. 20, pp. 437–61.

Hawkins, F. (1991) *Critical Years in Immigration: Canada and Australia Compared*, 2nd. ed. Montreal: McGill-Queen's University Press.

Hawkins, F. (1972) *Canada and Immigration: Public Policy and Public Concern*. Montreal: McGill-Queen's University Press.

Hess, M. (1991) "Sinful Wages" *Perception (Canadian Council on Social Development)*, vol. 15, no. 3, pp. 29–32.

Hill-Collins, P. (1990) *Black Feminist Thought: Knowledge, Consciousness, and the Politics of Empowerment*. London: Unwin Hyman.

Howe, N., and B. Strauss. (1993) *13th GEN: Abort, Retry, Ignore, Fail?* New York: Vintage Books.

Hughes, K.D. (1995) "Women in Non-traditional Occupations." *Perspectives on Labour and Income*, vol. 7, no. 3 (Autumn), pp. 14–19.

Hunter, A.A., and J. McKenzie Leiper. (1993) "On Formal Education, Skills and Earnings: The Role of Educational Certificates in Earnings Determination." *Canadian Journal of Sociology*, vol. 18, pp. 21–42.

Henry, F. (1994) *The Caribbean Diaspora in Toronto: Learning to Live with Racism*. Toronto: University of Toronto Press

Henry, F., C. Tator, W. Mattis, and T. Rees. (1995) *The Colour of Democracy: Racism in Canadian Society*. Toronto: Harcourt Brace.

Herrnstein, R., and C.A. Murray. (1994) *The Bell Curve: Intelligence and the Class Structure in American Life*. New York: Free Press.

Hiro, D. (1991) *Black British White British: A History of Race Relations in Britain*. London: Grafton Books.

House of Commons, Subcommittee Report. (1993) *Towards 2000: Eliminating Child Poverty*. Ottawa: Government Printers.

Jackson, C. (1996) "Measuring and Valuing Households' Unpaid Work." *Canadian Social Trends*, no. 42 (Autumn), Ottawa: Statistics Canada, pp. 25–29.

Jacobsson, R., and K. Alfredsson. (1993) *Equal Worth: The Status of Men and Women in Sweden*. Stockholm: Swedish Institute.

Jones, G. (1995) *Leaving Home*. Buckingham: Open University Press.

Johnson, L. (1979) *Precapitalist Economic Formations and the Capitalist Labour Market in Canada*, 2nd ed. Scarborough: Prentice-Hall.

Katz, M.B. (1975) *The People of Hamilton, Canada West: Family and Class in a Mid-Nineteenth-Century City*. Cambridge: Harvard University Press.

Keniston, K. (1975) "Prologue: Youth as a Stage of Life," in R. J. Havighurst and P.H. Dreyer (eds.), *Youth*. Chicago: University of Chicago Press.

Klein, H. (1990) "Adolescence, Youth, and Young Adulthood: Rethinking Current Conceptualizations of Life Stage." *Youth and Society*, vol. 21, pp. 446–71.

Lasch, C. (1977) *Haven in a Heartless World: The Family Besieged*. New York: Basic Books.

Lavoie, Y., and J. Oderkirk. (1993) "Social Consequences of Demographic Change." *Canadian Social Trends*, no. 31 (Winter), Ottawa: Statistics Canada, pp. 2–5.

Lee, D.E. (1996) *Generations and the Challenge of Justice*. Lanham: University Press of America.

Lengerman, P.M., and R.A. Wallace. (1985) *Gender in America: Social Control and Social Change*. Englewood Cliffs, NJ: Prentice-Hall.

Lewis, G.K. (1983) *Main Currents in Caribbean Thought*. Baltimore: Johns Hopkins University Press.

Li, P. (1988) *Ethnic Inequality in a Class Society*. Toronto: Wall and Thompson.

Li, P. (ed.) (1990) *Race and Ethnic Relations in Canada*. Toronto: Oxford University Press.

Lindsay, C., M.S. Devereaux, and M. Bergob. (1994) *Youth in Canada*, 2nd ed. Ottawa: Minister of Industry, Science and Technology.

Lipman-Blumen, J. (1984) *Gender Roles and Power*. Englewood Cliffs, NJ: Prentice-Hall.

Lips, H.M. (1991) *Women, Men, and Power*. Mountain View, CA: Mayfield.

Little, B. (1995) "Why It's Not So Wonderful to Be Young." *The Globe and Mail*, 9 Jan., p. A9.

Lockhart, A. (1978) *Future Failure: A Systematic Analysis of Changing Middle Class Opportunities in Canada*. University of Essex, Unpublished Doctoral Dissertation.

Lockhart, A. (1975) "Future Failure: The Unanticipated Consequences of Educational Planning," in E. Zureik and R.M. Pike (eds.), *Socialization and Values in Canadian Society*. Toronto: McClelland and Stewart, pp. 182–208.

Logan, R., and J. Belliveau. (1995) "Working Mothers." *Canadian Social Trends*, no. 36 (Spring), Ottawa: Statistics Canada, pp. 24–28.

Looker, E.D. (1994) "Active Capital: The Impact of Parents on Youths' Educational Performance and Plans," in L. Erwin and D. MacLennan (eds.), *Sociology of Education in Canada: Critical Perspectives on Theory, Research and Practice*. Toronto: Copp Clark Longman, pp. 164–187.

Macpherson, C.B. (1978) *Property: Mainstream and Critical Perspectives.* Toronto: University of Toronto Press.

Macpherson, C.B. (1973) *Democratic Theory: Essays in Retrieval.* London: Clarendon Press.

Macpherson, C.B. (1965) *The Real World of Democracy.* Toronto: CBC Enterprises.

Malarek, V. (1987) *Haven's Gate: Canada's Immigration Fiasco.* Toronto: Macmillan.

Males, M.A. (1996) *The Scapegoat Generation: America's War on Adolescents.* Monroe, Maine: Common Courage Press.

Marchak, M.P. (1988) *Ideological Perspectives on Canada*, 3rd ed. Toronto: McGraw-Hill Ryerson.

Marger, M. (1994) *Race and Ethnic Relations: American and Global Perspectives*, 3rd ed. Belmont, California: Wadsworth.

Marshall, K. (1994) "Balancing Work and Family Responsibilities." in *Perspectives on Labour and Income*, vol. 6, no. 1 (Spring), pp. 26–30.

Maslow, A.H. (1954) *Motivation and Personality.* New York: Harper and Row.

Mason, W. (1968) *The French Canadians, 1760–1945,* vol. 1. Toronto: Macmillan.

McDonald, L., and M.Y.T. Chen. (1993) "The Youth Freeze and the Retirement Bulge: Older Workers and the Impending Labour Shortage." *Journal of Canadian Studies*, vol. 28, pp. 75–101.

McKie, C. (1993) "Population Aging: Baby Boomers into the 21st Century." *Canadian Social Trends*, no. 29 (Summer) Ottawa: Statistics Canada, pp. 2–6.

McQuaig, L. (1987) *Behind Closed Doors: How the Rich Won Control of Canada's Tax System ... and Ended up Richer.* Markham, ON: Viking.

McVey, W.W. Jr., and W.E. Kalbach. (1995) *Canadian Population.* Toronto: Nelson.

Mead, M. (1950) *Male and Female: A Study of the Sexes in a Changing World.* Harmondsworth, Middlesex: Penguin.

Memmi, A. (1965) *The Colonizer and the Colonized.* Boston: Beacon Press.

Merser, C. (1987) *"Grown-ups": A Generation in Search of Adulthood.* New York: Putnam.

Miles, R. (1989) *Racism.* London: Routledge.

Modell, J., F.F. Furstenberg, and T. Hershberg. (1976) "Social Change and Transitions to Adulthood in Historical Perspective." *Journal of Family History*, vol. 1, pp. 7–31.

Molyneux, M. (1986) "Mobilization without Emancipation? Women's Interests, State, and Revolution," in R.R. Fagen, C.D. Deere, and C.L. Corragio (eds.), *Transition and Development: Problems of Socialism in the Third World.* New York: Monthly Review, pp. 180–302.

Morch, S. (1995) "Culture and the Challenge of Adaptation: Foreign Youth in Denmark." *International Journal of Comparative Race & Ethnic Studies*, vol. 2, no. 1, pp. 102–15.

Morissette, R., J. Myles, and G. Picot. (1993) *What Is Happening to Earnings Inequality in Canada?* (Analytic studies branch research papers series No. 60). Ottawa: Statistics Canada.

Myles, J., W.G. Picot, and T. Wannell. (1988) *Wages and Jobs in the 1980s: Changing Youth Wages and the Declining Middle* (Analytic studies branch research papers series No. 17). Ottawa: Statistics Canada.

Nakhaie, M.R. (1995) "Ownership and Management Position of Canadian Ethnic Groups in 1973 and 1989." *The Canadian Journal of Sociology*, vol. 20, no. 2, pp. 167–92.

Newman, P.C. (1981) *The Canadian Establishment*, vol. 2. Toronto: McClelland and Stewart.

Newman, P.C. (1975) *The Canadian Establishment*, vol. 1. Toronto: McClelland and Stewart.

Nobert, L., and R. McDowell. (1994) *Profile of Post-Secondary Education in Canada: 1993 edition*. Ottawa: Ministry of Supply and Services.

Nobert, L., R. McDowell, and D. Goulet. (1992) *Profile of Higher Education in Canada: 1991 edition*. Ottawa: Ministry of Supply and Services.

Normand, J. (1995) "Education of Women in Canada." *Canadian Social Trends*, no. 39 (Winter), Ottawa: Statistics Canada, pp. 17–21.

Nourbese Philip, Marlene. (1995) "Signifying Nothing: Why the Media Have Fawned over Bissoondath's *Selling Illusions*." *Border/Lines*, no. 36, pp. 4–11.

Olzak, Susan. (1985) "Ethnicity and Theories of Ethnic Collective Behaviour" *Research in Social Movements, Conflicts and Change*. Vol. 8, pp. 65–85.

O'Neill, J. (1991) "Changing Occupational Structure" in *Canadian Social Trends*, no. 23 (Winter), Ottawa: Statistics Canada, pp. 8–12.

Orwell, G. (1949) *Nineteen Eighty-Four*. Harmondsworth, Middlesex: Penguin.

Palladino, G. (1996) *Teenagers: An American History*. New York: Basic Books.

Pammett, J. (1996) "Getting Ahead Around the World," in A. Frizzell and J.H. Pammett (eds.), *Social Inequality in Canada*. Ottawa: Carleton University Press, pp. 67–86.

Park, R.E. (1950) *Race and Culture*. Glencoe, Ill.: Free Press.

Parsons, T. (1953) "A Revised Analytical Approach to the Theory of Social Stratification," in T. Parsons, *Essays in Sociological Theory*. New York: Free Press, (1964), pp. 386–439.

Parsons, T. (1940) "An Analytical Approach to the Theory of Social Stratification," in T. Parsons, *Essays in Sociological Theory*. New York: Free Press, (1964), pp. 69–88.

Pettigrew, T.F. (1964) *A Profile of the Negro American*. New York: Van Nostrand.

Phillips, C.E. (1957) *The Development of Education in Canada.* Toronto: Gage.

Phillips, P., and E. Phillips. (1993) *Women and Work: Inequality in the Candian Labour Market.* Toronto: James Lorimer and Company.

Picot, G., and J. Myles. (1996) "Children in Low-Income Families." *Canadian Social Trends,* no. 42 (Autumn), Ottawa: Statistics Canada, pp. 15–19.

Picot, G., J. Myles, and T. Wannell. (1990) *Good Jobs/Bad Jobs and the Declining Middle: 1967–1986* (Analytic studies branch research papers series No. 28). Ottawa: Statistics Canada.

Pineo, P.C., and J.C. Goyder. (1973) "Social Class Identification of National Sub-Groups," in J.E. Curtis and W.G. Scott (eds.), *Social Stratification in Canada.* Scarborough: Prentice-Hall, pp. 187–96.

Pleck, E.H. (1993) "Gender Roles and Relations," in M.K. Cayton, E.J. Gorn, and P.W. Williams (eds.), *Encyclopedia of American Social History,* vol. 3. New York: Scribner's, pp. 1945–60.

Porter, J. (1965) *The Vertical Mosaic: An Analysis of Social Class and Power in Canada.* Toronto: University of Toronto Press.

Proefrock, D.W. (1981) "Adolescence: Social Fact and Psychological Concept." *Adolescence,* vol. 26 no. 64, pp. 851–58.

Rashid, A. (1994) "Changes in Real Wages." *Canadian Social Trends,* no. 30 (Spring), Ottawa: Statistics Canada, pp. 16–18.

Ravanera, Z.R. (1995) "A Portrait of the Family Life of Young Adults," in J. Dumas (ed.), *Family Over the Life Course: Current Demographic Analysis.* Ottawa: Ministry of Industry, pp. 27–35.

Reitz, J.G. (1990) "Ethnic Concentrations in Labour Markets and their Implications for Ethnic Inequality," in Raymond Breton et al., *Ethnic Identity and Equality: Varieties of Experience in a Canadian City.* Toronto: University of Toronto Press, pp. 146–95.

Rejai, M. (1991) *Political Ideologies: A Comparative Approach.* London: M.E. Sharpe.

Rejai, M. (1971) "Political Ideology: Theoretical and Comparative Perspectives," in M. Rejai (ed.), *Decline of Ideology.* Chicago: Aldine and Atherton, pp. 1–29.

Renaud, V., and J. Badets. (1993) "Ethnic Diversity in the 1990s." *Canadian Social Trends,* no. 30 (Autumn), Ottawa: Statistics Canada, pp. 17–20.

Richmond, A.H. (1994) *Global Apartheid: Refugees, Racism, and the New World Order.* Toronto: Oxford University Press.

Rifkin, J. (1995) *The End of Work.* New York: Putman's.

Rose, S. (1979) "'It's Only Human Nature': The Sociobiologist's Fairyland." *Race and Class,* vol. 20, no. 3, pp. 277–87.

Ross, D.P., E.R. Shillington, and C. Lochhead. (1994) *The Canadian Fact Book on Poverty, 1994.* Ottawa, Ontario: Canadian Council on Social Development.

Rushton, J.P. (1995) *Race, Evolution and Behaviour: A Lifehistory Perspective.* New Brunswick, NJ: Transaction Publishers.

Russell, J.W. (1994) *After the Fifth Sun: Class and Race in North America.* Englewood Cliffs, NJ: Prentice-Hall.

Sanday, P.R. (1981) *Female Power and Male Dominance: On the Origins of Sexual Inequality.* Cambridge: Cambridge University Press.

Sarlo, C.A. (1992) *Poverty in Canada.* Vancouver: Fraser Institute.

Sartre, J.P. (1965) "Introduction" to Albert Memmi's *The Colonizer and the Colonized.* Boston: Beacon Press.

Sartre, J.P. (1963) "Preface" to *The Wretched of the Earth* (Franz Fanon). New York: Grove Press.

Satzewich, V.N. (1992) *Deconstructing a Nation: Immigration, Multiculturalism and Racism in 90s Canada.* Halifax: Fernwood.

Saunders, D. (1996) "Graduates Facing Postponed Beginnings." *Globe and Mail,* 22 April, pp. A1 and A8.

Scott, B. (1996) "Canadian Public Perceptions of Inequality Directions and Policy Implications," in A. Frizzell and J.H. Pammett (eds.), *Social Inequality in Canada.* Ottawa: Carleton University Press, pp. 87–106.

Singer, B. (1986) *Advertising and Society.* Don Mills, ON: Addison-Wesley.

Singh Bolaria, B., and P.S. Li. (1988) *Racial Oppression in Canada,* 2nd ed. Toronto: Garamond.

Statistics Canada. (1995a) *Women in Canada: A Statistical Report,* 3rd ed. Ottawa: Ministry of Industry.

Statistics Canada. (1995b) *Historical Labour Force Statistics.* Cat. 71-201. 1991 Census. Ottawa: Supply and Services Canada.

Statistics Canada. (1992a) *Income Distribution by Size in Canada, 1992.* Cat. No. 13-207. Ottawa: Supply and Services Canada.

Statistics Canada. (1992b) *Age, Sex and Marital Status.* 1991 Census of Canada. Catalogue number 93-310. Ottawa: Supply and Services Canada.

Statistics Canada. (1991a) *Industry and Class of Worker.* Cat. 93-326. 1991 Census. Ottawa: Supply and Services Canada.

Statistics Canada. (1991b) *Labour Force Activity.* Cat. 93-324. 1991 Census. Ottawa: Supply and Services Canada.

Statistics Canada. (1991c) *Population and Dwelling Count.* Cat. 93-304. Census. Ottawa: Supply and Services Canada.

Statistics Canada. (1991d) *Employment Income by Occupation.* Cat. 93-332. Census. Ottawa: Supply and Services Canada.

Statistics Canada. (1984) *Self-Employment in Canada.* Cat. 71-582. Ottawa: Supply and Services Canada.

Statistics Canada. (1982) *Age, Sex and Marital Status.* 1981 Census of Canada. Catalogue number 92-902. Ottawa: Supply and Services Canada.

Steele, S. (1990) *The Content of Our Character: A New Vision of Race in America.* New York: Harper and Collins.

Sunter, D. (1994a) "Youths — Waiting It Out." *Perspectives on Labour and Income*, vol. 6, no. 1 (Spring), pp. 31–36.

Sunter, D. (1994b) "The Labour Market: Mid-year Review" *Perspectives on Labour and Income*, vol. 6, no. 3 (Autumn), pp. 2–10.

Swedish Institute. (1992) *Equality Between Men and Women in Sweden.* Stockholm: Author.

Synge, J. (1979) "The Transition from School to Work: Growing Up in Early 20th-Century Hamilton, Ontario," in K. Ishwaran (ed.). *Childhood and Adolescence in Canada.* Toronto: McGraw-Hill Ryerson, pp. 246–69.

Teeple, G. (1995) *Globalization and the Decline of Social Reform.* Toronto: Garamond.

Turner, B.S. (1986) *Equality.* Chichester, Sussex: Ellis Horwood.

United Nations Development Project (UNDP). *Human Development Report.* (1992–1997) New York: Oxford University Press.

Vallières, P. (1971) *White Niggers of America.* Toronto: McClelland and Stewart.

Veltmeyer, H. (1987) *Canadian Corporate Power.* Toronto: Garamond.

Veltmeyer, H. (1986) *Canadian Class Structure.* Toronto: Garamond.

Wannell, T., and N. Caron. (1994) *The Gender Earnings Gap among Recent Postsecondary Graduates, 1984–92* (Analytic studies branch research paper series No. 68). Ottawa: Statistics Canada.

Wente, M. (1995) "What a Woman Earns, Then and Now." *Globe and Mail*, 11 Feb., p. A2.

White, L. (1994) "Co-residence and Leaving Home: Young Adults and Their Parents." *Annual Review of Sociology*, vol. 20, pp. 81–102.

William T. Grant Foundation. (1988) *The Forgotten Half: Non-College Youth in America.* Washington: Author.

Wolpe, H. (1986) "Class Concepts, Class Struggle, and Racism," in J. Rex and D. Mason (eds.), *Theories of Race and Ethnic Relations.* Cambridge: Cambridge University Press, pp. 110–30.

Wright, E.O. (1994) *Interrogating Inequality: Essays on Class Analysis, Socialism, and Marxism.* London: Verso.

Wright, E.O. (1985) *Classes.* London: Verso.

Wright, E.O. (1976) "Class Boundaries in Advanced Capitalist Societies." *New Left Review*, vol. 98, pp. 3–41.

Wright, E.O., and L. Perrone. (1977) "Marxist Class Categories and Income Equality." *American Sociological Review*, vol. 42 (February), pp. 32–55.

Yinger, J.M. (1981) "Toward a Theory of Assimilation and Dissimilation." *Ethnic and Racial Studies*, vol. 4, pp. 249–64.

PRINTED AND BOUND
IN BOUCHERVILLE, QUÉBEC, CANADA
BY MARC VEILLEUX IMPRIMEUR INC.
IN MARCH, 1998